D0040710

Life is Good

Life is Good

THE BOOK

How to Live with Purpose & Enjoy the Ride

BERT and JOHN JACOBS

☐ NATIONAL GEOGRAPHIC

WASHINGTON, D.C.

Published by the National Geographic Society
1145 17th Street NW Washington, DC 20036

Library of Congress Cataloging-in-Publication Data

Jacobs, Bert, 1964-
Life is good : the book / Bert and John Jacobs.
pages cm ISBN 978-1-4262-1563-6 (hardback)
1. Jacobs, Bert, 1964- 2. Jacobs, John, 1968- 3. Life Is Good (Firm) 4. Clothing
trade--United States. 5. Businesspeople--United States--Conduct of life. 6. Optimism. I. Jacobs, John, 1968- II. Title.
HD9940.U6L5553 2015
650.1--dc23

2015020909

The National Geographic Society is one of the world's largest nonprofit scientific
and educational organizations. Its mission is to inspire people to care about the
planet. Founded in 1888, the Society is member supported and offers a community
for members to get closer to explorers, connect with other members, and help make
a difference. The Society reaches more than 450 million people worldwide each
month through *National Geographic* and other magazines; National Geographic
Channel; television documentaries; music; radio; films; books; DVDs; maps; exhibi-
tions; live events; school publishing programs; interactive media; and merchandise.
National Geographic has funded more than 10,000 scientific research, conser-
vation, and exploration projects and supports an education program promoting
geographic literacy. For more information, visit www.nationalgeographic.com.

National Geographic Society
1145 17th Street NW
Washington, DC 20036-4688 USA

Your purchase supports our nonprofit work and makes you part of our global community. Thank you for sharing our belief in the power of science, exploration, and
storytelling to change the world. To activate your member benefits, complete your
free membership profile at natgeo.com/joinnow.

For information about special discounts for bulk purchases, please contact National
Geographic Books Special Sales: ngspecsales@ngs.org

For rights or permissions inquiries, please contact National Geographic Books
Subsidiary Rights: ngbookrights@ngs.org

Interior design: Melissa Farris

Printed in the United States of America

15/QGT-CML/1

For our mom,
Joan Jacobs,
who showed us that
being an optimist
is not only fun—
it's powerful.

*All illustrations in this book are the work
of the Life is Good Creative Team, and represent
more than 25 years of original artwork.*

CONTENTS

Life
is Good®

Life is not easy.
Life is not perfect.
Life is good.

Who are we to declare that life is good? Good question. We're two ordinary brothers from Boston who didn't want a real job but weren't afraid to work. After graduating college, we decided we wanted to make a living by creating art. Designing and selling T-shirts seemed like a fun, simple way to take a shot at starting a business.

Today, Life is Good is a $100 million clothing company with one simple, unifying mission: to spread the power of optimism. Art in all its forms remains our essential ingredient and primary vehicle for communicating our positive messages. Known for our clothing (T-shirts, in particular), we continue to embrace new canvases, mediums, and collaborations that enable us to inspire more people. A minimum of 10 percent of our annual profits goes to helping kids overcome poverty, violence, and severe medical challenges. Our nonprofit foundation, The Life is Good Kids Foundation, positively impacts the lives of more than 100,000 children a day.

When we started back in 1989, we had no experience, but we were game for an adventure. We bought a used minivan, tore out the backseats, and called it "The Enterprise," telling each other we would "boldly go where no T-shirt guys had gone before." For five years, we drove The Enterprise up and down the East Coast, selling our T-shirts in the streets and door-to-door in college dorms. We lived on peanut butter and jelly, slept in the van, and showered when we could. The ladies were not impressed.

By 1994, with a combined total of $78 to our names, we were considering giving up on the ultimate road trip. But one highway conversation about the daily flood of negative news led to one idea that led to one shirt that led to one brand, called Life is Good.

Those three words changed our lives forever. We continued to stumble forward, making mistakes left and right—but the power of that one idea was too strong for even us to screw up. Customers embraced the brand and took its simple yet powerful message to heart. Although we had no idea what a business plan was (we once asked our bookkeeper if mountain bikes were tangible assets), the business grew because people were craving something positive amid the steady storm of doom and gloom.

And—then as now—our customers helped to plot our course for the long haul. We started getting mail from optimists celebrating the simple things that made their lives good. Unexpectedly, we also started receiving many letters and emails from people fighting to overcome great adversity, like cancer and the loss of loved ones. Their courageous stories demonstrated how optimism can empower us even in the hardest times. We were inspired and moved by all of these stories, which we started calling "Fuel." But we never knew what to do with them—until it occurred to us to *share* them. That's when a growing tribe began to rally around Life is Good's deeper meaning.

Why Optimism?

Optimism is not just a philosophical viewpoint. It's not irrational cheerfulness, and it's not blind positivity. Optimism is a powerful and pragmatic strategy for accomplishing goals and living a fulfilling life. By acknowledging obstacles and opportunities—but focusing on the opportunities—optimism enables us to explore the world with open arms and an eye toward solutions, progress, and growth. It also makes life a hell of a lot more fun.

Fortunately, over the past 20 years, the benefits of optimism have been validated by a large, growing body of scientific research. Studies have demonstrated a strong link between optimism and increased mental and physical health, greater resilience in the face of stress and adversity, and a higher overall quality of life.

The choice of optimism opens our minds to infinite possibilities. We all get one wild ride on this beautiful planet, right? How are you spending your time? Are you doing what you love? Are you loving what you do? When you look back on your life, will you feel you made the most of it? Those are big questions for all of us, and they can be both exciting and daunting.

The Life is Good Superpowers

Optimism does much more than beat the alternative. It enables us to access the ten most important tools we have for living a happy and fulfilling life. We call them the Life is Good Superpowers. But unlike X-ray vision, bullet speed, or Herculean strength, they are accessible to us all.

The Life is Good superpowers will help you overcome obstacles, drive forward with greater purpose, and enjoy the ride of life.

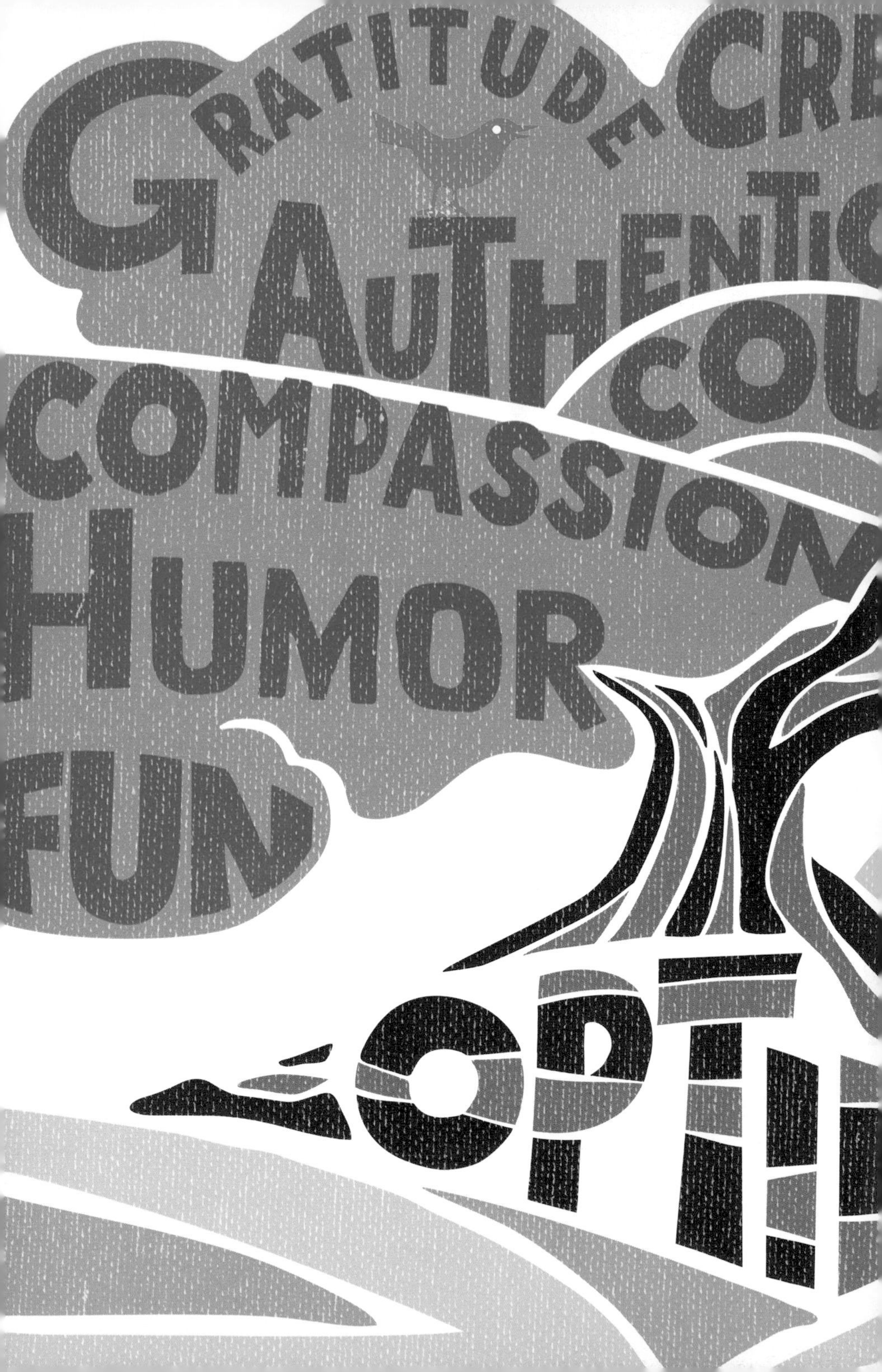
GRATITUDE
COMPASSION
HUMOR
FUN

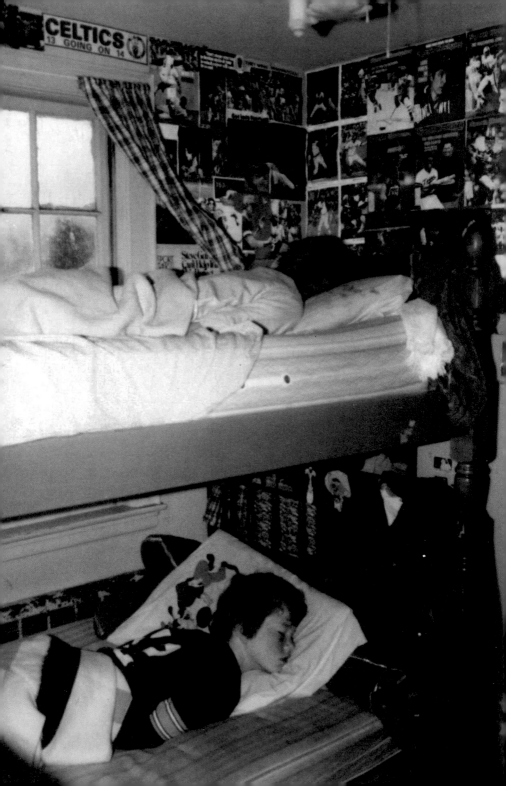

Scallywags

Our perfectly imperfect childhood would be our introduction to the power of optimism, and the beginnings of Life is Good—long before we knew it.

We are the two youngest of six kids. We grew up in a chaotic, lower-middle-class home in a beautiful town called Needham, just outside Boston. The house originally measured 720 square feet. After the first few babies showed up, our father, Al Jacobs, built a second floor virtually by himself, bumping the total square footage up to 1,260 for the eight of us. Dad reasoned that the second floor (where the first four kids slept and the windows iced on the inside) needed no heating system because "heat rises, and you kids hang out mostly downstairs in the winter." That little house was full of action, banter, and enough dysfunction to make good theater for all our friends.

Our dad, a World War II and Korean War Air Force veteran, was born in 1921. He worked on electronics and radar equipment at a navigation company. His passions for precise machinery, semiconductors, astronomy, aviation, and many other topics flew clear over our young heads. He was able to transmit a strong appreciation for the outdoors to his kids, taking us camping and leading us on hikes and canoe trips. Even on the trail, he always emphasized the importance of taking our time to eat together. Early on our parents made ends meet, but by the time their last two sons arrived, both their funds and their sanity had been understandably stretched beyond reason. They had bitten off a lot trying to raise a family of six kids on a slim salary.

Bert (top bunk) and John catching z's circa 1978.
Sports were big; sheets were overrated.

Joan, our mom, managed the daily circus on the home front. Each morning, she would grab a saucepan and start banging on it with a metal spoon. "Wake up, you scallywags!" she'd shout as we slowly rolled out of our bunk beds.

As we downed breakfast, Mom would be busy making all our school lunches. Her daily production was a model of efficiency. Every day, lunch was six PB and Js on white Wonder Bread with Welch's grape jelly and six red apples. Six brown bags were labeled with our names in cursive #2 pencil (in order of appearance)—Eileen, Auberta, Eddie, Allan, Bert, and John. Joan made it clear to us all: "Fold and save your brown bag to reuse if you want lunch again tomorrow."

HOW JOAN'S UNCOMMON SENSE FED THE FAMILY

- "I like running out of money; then I don't have to worry about what I need to buy."
- "I buy the cereals you don't like because they last longer."
- (Insisting a blueberry pie was not a blueberry pie): "It's an apple pie. I just ran out of apples."

Joan was no award-winning chef. But before you criticize her culinary skills, consider the facilities. The kitchen at 11 Sunnyside Road was built to the exact specifications of a phone booth. Joan claimed to love it because she "could reach everything from one spot." Our mom knew how to wing it ("Hunger is the best sauce," she'd always say) and how to sing it ("Yes, we have no bananas!")— any song that kept our taste buds distracted and team spirits high.

On his payday, Al would treat us all to pizza night. Sometimes four or five of us would cram in the car for the pickup, just to smell the fresh pies straight out of the oven from Gino's Pizza. It was festive in the packed dining room, and friends knew it as a great evening to partake in the madness.

Life Is Not Perfect

When we were in elementary school, our parents were in a near-death car accident. Mom escaped with only broken bones, but Dad almost had his right arm amputated and lost the use of his right

Al Jacobs takes his four oldest kids for an afternoon hike in the mid-1960s.

hand permanently. He had always been a talented, idealistic crafts-man and a devout lover of the great outdoors. It's hard to overstate the impact of that accident.

Admirably, he powered through rehabilitation, and although his body would never be the same, he was quickly back to work and putting food on the table. But the frustration from his physical limitations compounded his mounting stress, and the pressure in the house was palpable. Our friends secretly nicknamed him The Bear because of his frightening habit of bursting out of his cave growling with one big paw raised. As Dad's temper grew harsher, his screaming and yelling became a dominant daily sound track in our lives.

The house itself began to deteriorate as well. The front gutter rotted on the ground all winter as we chopped away the ice on the front steps. Grass grew wildly and uncut for months at a time. Garage windows remained broken for years. Books and random boxes piled up inside the house. The tension at home would peak each month when bills were due, and anything (from Mom to us kids to stray objects left on the floor) could be the target of The Bear's next outburst. In retrospect, it's clear that Al was yelling at himself and not us—but at the time, we were far from understanding that. We did our best to combat or deflect the anger away from Joan and each other, but the rages became part of our shared reality.

There were days when Joan openly questioned her own capabilities. "I don't know why anyone thought I was capable of being a mother," she would say. That was hard to hear from our own mom. Her resilient, joyful spirit was repeatedly tested. Never broken, but often tested.

The Jacobses were never mistaken for the Kennedys. Clockwise from top left: Auberta, Eileen, Eddie, Bert, John, and Allan.

Frequent Flyers

The erosion of reliable structure at home both challenged and benefited us as the two youngest kids. It was embarrassing not being able to afford cleats for football or baseball, or being left without a

John enjoys downtime at Cricket Field in the early 1970s.

ride home after practice. But on the other hand, we had a lot more freedom than most kids. We had freedom to play, to explore, and to develop our own ideas about the world around us. We shared bunk beds together, played Wiffle Ball together, laughed together, and stuck by each other.

When we were toddlers, Joan sat us on the kitchen floor and suggested things for us to draw (flying submarines, superheroes, ballplayers, UFOs) as she pivoted around us, concocting and cleaning from her command center. A talented artist, she challenged us to invent stories and scenes beyond what the "boob tube" could offer. Glenn Miller or Johnny Cash played on, but the TV stayed off.

Our mom was the first powerful optimist in our lives. We weren't the kind of family that could fly to Disneyland on vacation, but Joan taught us how to travel in our minds. She didn't just read us bedtime stories at night; she sang to us, danced, and acted out the stories. She became the pirate or the queen or the wolf. And we loved it! She unlocked our imaginations. Could there be a greater gift? We would beg for more and more adventures. She took us sailing in forbidden seas, brought us up the marble steps of the grandest castles, and wandered with us deep into lush, enchanted forests. She filled that little old house with light, music, love, and her wild, infectious laughter.

> It is important to remember that we all have magic inside us.
> —J. K. Rowling

Snow days with Joan were always a special treat. Most parents probably worried about safety or the traffic reports, but not our mom. She'd come flying into our room more excited than any of the kids: "School is canceled today! Yippeeee!!!" And then she'd suit up with us and go sledding. She knew a snow day was like Christmas for us, and she might as well have been Santa.

Free-Range Humans

When we were kids, Joan and Al cut us loose to explore the great mysteries of our neighborhood: climbing oaks, the "jungle" woods, the strange swamp that served as a giant sandbox, with monster dirt hills and murky moats. Across the street was the most improbable of all prizes: Cricket Field. Somehow, for $15,000 in 1959, our parents had landed a house about 30 feet away from Fenway Park, the Olympic Village, or whatever we decided that field was on a given day. That sprawling patch of green (or white in the winter) was heaven on earth to us. Any game was possible: Kick the Can, Capture the Flag, snow football. Joan and Al never took issue with our filthy, ripped clothes; they were natural by-products of a liberating (read: necessary) parenting style that encouraged us to get out, get dirty, and make our own fun.

When night fell, Joan would pop out on the front steps and ring her dinner bell, belting out "Tiiiiime for dinnerrrrr!" No matter where we were, we could hear that thing ring. And thanks to Joan and Al, any friend or stranger was welcome at any hour. Sometimes our siblings' friends would just climb up on the garage, hop onto the house roof, and crawl in an upstairs window. That classic dinner bell ritual organized the chaos. Just as the mosquitos came out, all the mangy Jacobs kids rolled in.

Tell Me Something Good

Probably the most valuable gift Joan ever gave her two girls and four boys was the simple request she made every night at the dinner table. There were often difficult things happening around the house. Maybe The Bear was in a bad mood. Maybe a police cruiser was outside looking for one of our older brothers (they weren't bad guys; they just didn't follow all the rules). She would look around at

all six of us with her smiling, squinting blue eyes and say, "Tell me something good that happened today."

As simple as Mom's words were, they changed the energy in the room. Before we knew it, we were all riffing on the best, funniest, or most bizarre part of our day:

"Allan got a funky buzz cut today! The barber wouldn't cut it long so he ran out halfway through. Check it out: It's a Whoa-hawk!"

"Did you see the time-travel spacebox Ed made? We can go into the future!"

"We found The Stones *Hot Rocks* album at the dump—only one side's scratched!"

Somehow, we were all laughing and connecting and acting like a tight-knit family. Joan's simple prompt made all the difference in the world. Rather than complaining about the day, commiserating about struggles, or opening up the possibility of a fight, she focused everyone on the positive. That optimism was something that our family always had, even when we had little else.

Eventually we became conscious of the fact that joy doesn't come from your circumstances. It comes from your disposition. This deep-rooted belief would only grow stronger as we became adults. Even at our worst moments, we've always had the tools that we needed to survive because of Mom. She showed us that optimism is a courageous choice you can make every day, especially in the face of adversity.

She was truly the inspiration for Life is Good.

Joan rocks the early grunge look at Mount Katahdin, Maine.

SUPERPOWER #1

NESS

Open your mind.

Youth Knows No Age

Mariana is a good friend of ours who lives nearby in Boston. A few years back she and her four-year-old son, Ernesto, went out for lunch at a local park. As they sat down at a picnic table and she began laying out some sandwiches and fruit, she noticed an old woman seated at another table not far from theirs. Her clothing looked shabby, and her bag was a bit dirty, so Mariana made the quick assumption that the woman was unstable.

Before she could stop him, her son jumped off the bench and ran to the woman. "Hi, I'm Ernesto!" he said.

"Well, hello, Ernesto," the woman said. "My name is Kate. It's a beautiful day, isn't it?"

Mariana stood up to chase down her son, thinking this woman could be dangerous. But now she wasn't so sure what to do. The woman sounded so healthy and well spoken. Mariana slowly sat back down, but kept watching closely.

"How old are you, Ernesto?" said Kate.

"Guess!" Ernesto shot back with a big smile. He was fascinated by Kate, staring at her long, wild gray hair.

Kate smiled back at Ernesto and said, "You look big enough to be five. Are you five years old?"

"Nope," he said, "I'm four. How old are you?"

"Guess!" she said. That surprised him, so the two of them started laughing.

Now Mariana was relaxing. "This woman isn't dangerous," she thought. "She's fun."

Ernesto had been challenged with a difficult question. He looked over to his mom for help, but she made it clear that he was on his own. He walked all around his new friend, looking her over very carefully. Finally, he cautiously touched the skin on her arm, and that seemed to inform his answer. He looked Kate right in the eyes and gave it his best shot: "A thousand?"

Mariana was mortified. But before she could apologize, the old woman threw her head back and burst out laughing. And once she started laughing hard—we all know how this goes—Ernesto started laughing too. Soon, Mariana had joined the club. Kate ended up joining them for lunch, and has since become a treasured friend of the family.

We were all children once, and we lived our lives with arms wide open. As we grow older, we sometimes grow more cynical and guarded. We catch ourselves being more closed-minded, which prevents us from exploring opportunities.

> May you stay forever young.
> —Bob Dylan

Children possess an abundance of the superpower we call openness. They inspire us with their active imaginations and their eagerness to greet the new, the strange, and the unfamiliar. Children can also show us how to express ourselves more freely, if we let them. And they can show us how to explore the world with open arms, embracing new experiences with unrestrained joy.

Yes, And . . .

If you've ever marveled at the lightning-quick, nimble minds of comedians like Tina Fey, Bill Murray, Amy Poehler, or Stephen Colbert—all who were mentored at one time by legendary improv pioneer Del Close—you may have seen a method to their collective madness. And that method is something we can all learn from.

Rule number one of improv comedy is the principle of "Yes, and." When they're collaborating onstage, improv actors never reject each other's ideas. They say, "Yes, and . . ." to accept and build upon each new contribution. There's no time to negate or judge an idea if the shared goal is to propel a scene forward and make something new. So you roll with whatever is served. It's about letting ideas breathe, trusting each other, and going on a journey of the unknown together.

Have you ever tried to brainstorm with someone who "brain-stomps" on every idea without giving it a chance? It's easier to knock something down than it is to build it up. But remember: The people who knock everything down never build anything. A quick "No" stops the flow. "Yes, and" lets you build and grow. This principle applies well beyond theater and comedy.

In 1980, we were in ninth and sixth grades when an NBA rookie named Larry Bird (aka The Hick from French Lick) breathed new life into an ailing Boston Celtics franchise. As his rivalry with L.A. Lakers great Earvin "Magic" Johnson took shape, it was a special time to be sports-crazed teenagers in Boston. For us, Bird's nightly miracles on the court ignited a burning desire to have a basketball hoop in our own driveway.

We pitched the idea hard to our mom, but she brought up some legitimate hurdles. For one, the driveway was too small and also made of gravel so the ball wouldn't bounce well. As she dished out oatmeal, she also emphasized that we had no money to pay for a new hoop. All good points.

Our brother Ed managed to flip the switch. "You're right about the gravel, Mom," Ed replied calmly. "That's why we want to set up the hoop in the street where it's smooth and there's plenty of space." John took it from there: "And there's already a telephone pole out there—we'll just use that." Bert chimed in that the pole had a street-light on it to boot, so we could play at night.

With Ed leading, our little three-man weave drill was working. He explained that he could build an adjustable hoop out of some angle iron from the basement; we knew we could find a discarded rim and backboard somewhere. Before we knew it, even Mom was joining in: "And I guess this way it could be for the whole neighborhood, right?"

Momentum is a powerful thing. Ed was always pretty handy with mechanical things, so two weeks later, our hoop dream was realized. Our collective "Yes, and" mindset would translate to countless hours of practice and good times with friends in the decade to come. Yes, and . . . Bird and Magic's legendary battles and team-first attitudes throughout the 1980s played a major role in reviving America's passion for pro basketball.

There's No Place Like Roam

At the crossroads of an important decision, it's hard to resist drawing quick conclusions and darting to answers. But if you can, first allow yourself the luxury of relaxing and exploring your options. This is not about being lazy; it's about understanding the nature of the human mind. Whether you are considering a new relationship, building a business plan, or building a tree fort in the backyard, take it slow and have some fun considering all the possibilities. A little bit of floundering and stumbling are, in fact, essential to the creative process.

Joan and Al's "hands-off parenting" at 11 Sunnyside Road trained us well in the arts of floundering and stumbling. In our early 20s, the question "What am I going to do with my life?" was top of mind for each of us. East Coast guys our entire lives, we both ventured out to

the Wild West in 1988. Bert had graduated from Villanova University the year before and was now putting his degree in communications to good use as an eloquent pizza delivery guy in a Colorado ski town. John was majoring in Wiffle Ball and English at California State in Chico, on exchange from the University of Massachusetts. Eager to see more of the grand old USA, we met up in Chico in full Jack Kerouac mode and began a meandering seven-week road trip that would weave across the country and bring us back to Beantown.

TEN GREAT ROAD TRIP SONGS

- "Glory Bound" Martin Sexton
- "Willin'" Little Feat
- "Stickshifts and Safetybelts" Cake
- "Radar Love" Golden Earring
- "On the Road Again" Willie Nelson
- "Going Up the Country" Canned Heat
- "Miracle Mile" Cold War Kids
- "Ramblin' Man" The Allman Brothers Band
- "Thunder Road" Bruce Springsteen
- "Wagon Wheel" Old Crow Medicine Show

We began with a thin stack of cash, a map of the United States, some mix tapes custom-made by our big brother Allan, and a strict plan of no plan. Openness is an essential ingredient to any great road trip.

One of our earliest discoveries on that map was Feather River, near the aptly named town of Paradise, California. Thanks to tips from locals, we found some amazing cliffs tucked into the woods, where we did our best running Butch and Sundance plunges into the crystal clear water far below.

Every leap involved two extended yelps: one ("Ahhhhhhhhhh-hhh!") on the way down, and one ("Yeaaaaaaaaaaaaah!") after confirming we were both still alive. It was pure magic, and it set the stage for a summerlong (and lifelong) pursuit of the perfect swimming hole, rope swing, or diving catch. For the remainder of the trip, blue water in any shape became our North Star. We didn't always know where we were, and we definitely didn't know where we were going, but we were enjoying the ride.

Bert tries to fly somewhere in northern California.

Whether we were in the mountains of Wyoming, cornfields of Nebraska, or streets of Chicago, we were gaining new perspectives and expanding our horizons. We didn't talk about it for weeks at a time, but that big question was still looming for both of us: "What am I going to do with my life?"

NOT ALL WHO

WANDER

ARE LOST

The grand landscapes, the characters we met, the great tunes, and the odd books (like *The Iowa Baseball Confederacy*) that we'd read aloud (shotgun rider to driver) by the dim overhead light as we rambled along: It all freed our minds to think about what mattered most, and gave us permission to think big.

John (left) and Bert living large in Los Angeles, summer of 1989

By the time we recrossed the Mississippi, ideas of hatching a business together back East were flowing. Rolling down the Massachusetts Turnpike on the tail end of our trip, a loose plan was coming into view. The dream was to build a business together that would allow us to make a living being creative. We talked about T-shirts as a financially accessible way to share art and messages. Starting our business would require no experience, no professional skills, and no money. Fortunately, we were qualified.

FUEL:
OPENNESS

Dear LIG,

On December 26th, I left Poland on a one-way ticket, with a childhood friend, 35 pounds on my back, and a wide-open plan. It was my dream since I was 15 years old, and after 10 years of just dreaming I was about to start the adventure of a lifetime. An adventure that lasted 360 days, and during which I traveled almost 40,000 miles. An adventure that changed my life, and during which "Do what you love. Love what you do" finally became reality.

I hitchhiked through Mexico and sailed along the Belizean coast; I climbed an active volcano in Guatemala and biked down another one in Ecuador; I scuba dived in the Bay Islands and West Indies, surfed with sea lions in the Galápagos, and walked through the Amazonian jungle. I learned to kitesurf in Brazil and ate termites and guinea pigs; I danced salsa, punta, and forro . . .

I volunteered at a kids' shelter in Peru, and worked at a bar in La Paz. I saw a Brazil vs. Chile soccer game, biked down the Death Road, and witnessed a cocaine smuggler being arrested. I participated in shamanic ceremonies in Colombia, and went rafting in Honduras. "Optimism can take you anywhere" was the motto of our trip, especially when we climbed Huayna Potosi (20,000-foot mountain).

This was the best year in my life—filled with sun, delicious food, challenge, freedom, laughter, hope, new friendships, and shooting stars! So when the trip came to an end, I knew I couldn't go back to the life I used to lead. I had to do what I love, and love what I do. And I had to do it with my partner in crime, my travel buddy, my best friend. We are opening a travel-oriented restaurant this summer, and we couldn't be happier because our Life is Good.

**Thank you,
Olga**

THREE WAYS TO STAY OPEN

1. **FOLLOW THE LEADER.** The next time you sit down with a child, imagine the child is your teacher. Let her tell you about the drawing or the toy, or where the story goes next. Let her show you her view of the world, in her own words. Follow her lead. Be willing to be silly, and let go of trying to direct the kid. You ask the "Whys?" and discover the world as she directs the kid in you.

2. **"YES, AND."** Try using this phrase wherever you work or meet in groups. Invite people to share their wildest ideas up front and encourage the group to take each one for a spin, accepting and building on it. The filtering and editing down can happen later, but this first crucial step creates an open environment of collaboration that sparks innovation. In your personal life, "Yes, and" will help foster a more adventurous, creative approach as well. Your mate wants to take a class, see a film, reboot a hobby, or take a spontaneous trip with you? In all cases, before you fall into the list of logical reasons why it may *not* make sense, try taking the open road of "Yes, and . . . I could join you. Let's take an art or cooking class together!" Let it breathe, expand on it, and enjoy that ride.

3. **EVERYTHING IS A ONCE-IN-A-LIFETIME EXPERIENCE.** Get out and see the world! We're not necessarily talking adventure travel (Olga all over if you can!) or long road trips (highly recommended as well). "If you don't go, you don't see" can also apply to your neighbor's home, a live show, a place you've been meaning to volunteer, or the contemporary art exhibit you're not quite sure is for you. Changing up your routine and physical surroundings will help open up your mind to fresh perspectives.

Of course, travel doesn't have to be physical. The imagination is a spaceship, and travel of the mind is free. Try reading books and watching films outside your go-to genre. Ask a music-loving friend, or tap into your favorite streaming service to refresh your personal playlist. Write your own outrageous story about the adventures that lie ahead for you and your loved ones. The bottom line is that it takes a conscious effort to step outside of your comfort zone to experience new things. Whenever you take that step, you're good to grow.

Enjoy the ride.

SUPERPOWER #2

COUR

AGE

Soul Sisters

Our sister Auberta (aka "Berta") has always been the nurturing type—from patching up her little brothers' wounds to helping around the house to baking and gifting the world's greatest chocolate chip cookies to everyone she knows while working her way through college. She chipped in with her hard-earned money to replace worn-out home furniture for the family. Quite naturally, in her early 20s she became a registered nurse.

Always an athlete, Berta was on a ski trip in Vermont with our sister Eileen in 1988 when she had a devastating, life-altering ski accident that broke her neck, leaving her completely paralyzed. She was 28 years old.

> Having courage does not mean that we are unafraid. Having courage and showing courage mean we face our fears. We are able to say, "I have fallen, but I will get up."
> —*Maya Angelou*

In the immediate aftermath of the fall, Berta remembers Eileen asking, "Do you want me to untangle your legs?" and replying, "I don't even know where they are." When the ski patrolman arrived and asked her to squeeze his hand, she recalls, "I could not, and I knew I was in big trouble."

In the days that followed, Berta lay immobile in a hospital in northern Vermont. Her neck injury was so unstable that it was

Auberta (left, always in fashion) and Eileen (forever in blue jeans) Jacobs in Vermont, 1987

unsafe for her to be transported to Boston. Her doctor informed her it was unlikely she would ever walk again. Eileen knew Berta needed to be surrounded by love and support; she spread the word quickly, which resulted in a blizzard of cards, gifts, and friends filling up her hospital room. All visitors, including us, were given strict orders from Berta herself: "I don't want anyone coming in sad for me. I need laughs, not tears."

Lying alone, she fought the darkness of her situation and made a conscious decision.

"If I'm sad, my whole family will be sad," she thought. "It doesn't help me or anybody." It was hard and strange to rely on others for absolutely everything, even scratching her nose. She desperately craved good signs to focus on, and slowly they appeared. One day, she shrugged her shoulders, and a few days later she moved an arm. Many of us were gathered around her bed on the day Berta finally was able to move a toe on her right foot. She had been wishing it so hard, she said, that she wouldn't have believed it if we hadn't all pointed and erupted in celebration.

For five weeks, Berta had zero hand movement. But every day she spent in that hospital room, she focused on the good, on the progress, on doing a little bit more. She was fortunate to have an exceptional primary nurse named Betty, who went above and beyond normal duties—even visiting on her days off to brighten Berta's spirits.

Six weeks after the accident, Berta underwent a risky and complex seven-hour surgery to fuse and stabilize her spine. Its success allowed her to begin rehabilitation. She had to relearn how to do everything, including rolling over and crawling. With assistance, she was eventually able to stand and take a few steps. "That was REALLY exciting," she says now. That same day she was transferred to a rehab hospital in Boston.

"You have to look at the good things," she says. "It's OK to be sad sometimes. I'm not saying I didn't cry a lot back then. I did. It always felt good to let it all out. But then I'd turn the page and focus my thoughts on getting better."

Eileen and Auberta feeling great and grateful at Berta's benefit road race in 1988

In rehab Berta saw many people who had it worse than she did—a reminder of how lucky she was. Her hospital friends organized a five-kilometer run to raise funds for her living costs, and we followed suit with a fundraiser basketball tourney. Eileen was there by her sister's side in every way, transporting Berta where she needed to be, coordinating visits from friends, and sorting through all the bills.

Berta eagerly embraced her exercises, craving every possible sign of progress. "Every step of the way," she said, "I felt lucky."

Within two years, after fanatical dedication to rehab, Berta was not only walking, she was able to bicycle as well. Six months later, she went back to work as an outpatient nurse, helping others with similar hardships and living independently all the while.

To this day, Berta deals with significant daily challenges related to her accident. Her overall motion is limited, and her hands can be particularly frustrating. Yet she manages, through it all, to maintain her resilient, positive energy and lifelong focus on the well-being of others. When you see Berta, you get a bright smile, a warm hug, and then sincere, earnest questions about your life.

"I have a lot of setbacks," she says, "but I try to look at them as things that may ruin my hour, but not my day, or my week. Put 'em in the rearview mirror and keep looking forward. When that first doctor way back told me I was unlikely to walk, I swore at him in my head. I immediately thought of people who walk and run marathons after they're told that. You can't always believe one doctor or one medical report. I always feel like there are options, possibilities, even when you don't know what

TEN STRONG SONGS OF COURAGE

- "Hey World (Don't Give Up)" Michael Franti
- "Darlin' Do Not Fear" Brett Dennen
- "Hero" Family of the Year
- "Brave" Sara Bareilles
- "Moving Forward" Colony House
- "Failure" Martin Sexton
- "Carry On" fun.
- "Don't Look Back" Peter Tosh
- "Bottom of the Barrel" Amos Lee
- "Head Full of Doubt/Road Full of Promise" The Avett Brothers

they are. You just have to be open to them. I know I'm lucky, but I do believe the first thing you can do for yourself is *believe*."

A friend once told Berta that he could never maintain her attitude if put in the same circumstances. "I don't think I'd have the courage to face each day with a smile the way you do," he said.

"You don't think you can do a lot of things until you're faced with choices," she says. "What are my choices after the accident: smile or frown? If smile is the courageous choice, that's an easy one for me," she says with a big Berta grin.

Easy? Hardly. Courageous? For sure. Many of our Fuel letters over the years have come from people in similar situations to Berta's. Faced with tremendous obstacles, courageous people somehow find a reservoir of optimism to help them look forward and focus on the good.

The word "courage" comes from the Latin root for "heart." To proceed with courage is to speak and act from a core of truth at the heart of your being. In Berta's case, that accident has caused her a lot of pain and difficulties in life—but it couldn't take her beautiful smile because that smile is who she is.

Courage is a superpower.

Everyday Courage

It takes courage to adapt to and overcome great adversity, to stand up to an opponent, or to do the right thing. There's also courage of the smaller, everyday variety, like a shy child who simply raises her hand in class.

We often associate courage with strong, powerful creatures like lions, tigers, and bears. But it has just as much to do with butterflies—the butterflies in your gut, the ones you feel right before you do what you are afraid to do. Orville Wright didn't have a pilot's license, and Orville Redenbacher didn't have a popcorn license. But each had the courage to try.

Optimists are able to view rejection as an opportunity to adjust and improve, embracing the chance to learn, grow, and try again. Whether you're considering pursuing a promotion or asking out a secret crush, remember hockey great Wayne Gretzky's advice: "You miss one hundred percent of the shots you don't take."

> Opportunities multiply as they are seized.
> —*Sun Tzu*

First Steps

Our own beginnings with Life is Good were very much about overcoming the unknowns and facing our fears every day. We can't compare our challenges to those of our sister Berta, or those of the many brave people who have written us Fuel letters through the years. But there may be aspects of our scrappiest years that you'll find relatable and helpful on your own road trip of life.

Our cross-country ramble in 1989 had opened our minds and given us the inspiration to chase our dream of combining art with business. Once we were back East, we dove right into designing some T-shirts and started selling them in the streets of Boston. During John's senior year at UMass, he dashed back and forth from Amherst to Boston while Bert held down the fort. By spring 1990, we dubbed our fledgling business "Jacobs Gallery" to try to emphasize our original art.

At ages 25 and 22, in 1990, we both still felt and acted like college students, so we saw college dorms as natural places to blend in and take our new T-shirt designs for a spin. We'd print up a few dozen of a new concept, fill one large gray duffel bag each, and sell door-to-door in the dorms of schools like Boston College, Northeastern University, and Boston University.

Entering the great unknown of a new campus carrying our untested designs always required a big deep breath. The first steps are the hardest to take. Instant hit? Not even close. Promising sales? Nada. Positive feedback? Rarely. Accessible audience we liked and felt we could learn from? YES. The next five years would be a lot of trial, and even more error. But we were each riding alongside the one guy who could make the other one laugh during our most pathetic misadventures. Good thing too, because for the next decade we would share not only a business, but also a van, an apartment, and just about every waking hour together.

In the summer of 1990, like only the coolest college grads do, we moved back in with our parents. Many parents might discourage their children from continuing down a path when they aren't experiencing much success. Late at night when we walked in the door from selling, our dad would ask, "How'd yous do?" And despite our answer, he would enthusiastically encourage us to keep trying. Thanks, Dad.

To augment our paltry sales revenue from the dorms and the street, we solicited custom T-shirt design jobs as well. At one point, we circulated creative flyers offering custom work to a long list of local businesses. Our ratio of flyers distributed (70) to responses of any kind (0) was less than promising.

This complete failure was an early, healthy dose of reality. Our first orders, or wins of any kind, would be the hardest to come by. Without any professional portfolio or references or track record, we

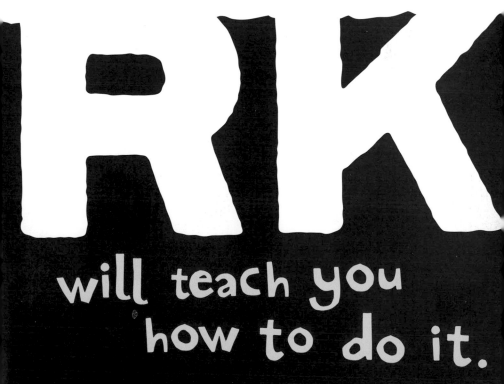

would need a triple shot of hustle and some thick skin to move forward. Sometimes you have to work to curb the fear of failure with an excited anticipation of the unknown. You have to fight to stay curious and optimistic. The early signs were not encouraging, but we did our best to focus on the adventure ahead. We got down, but we wouldn't let ourselves both get down at the same time. If one guy was dragging, the other would pick him up.

FIVE INSPIRING VEHICLES OF OPTIMISM

- The Bluesmobile
- The *Wright Flyer*
- Apollo 11
- The DeLorean Time Machine
- The Yellow Submarine

The Enterprise

Once we learned the rhythms of Boston-area dormitory sales' peaks and valleys, we went to a local library and mapped out a plan to be *somewhere* on a college campus selling our T-shirts virtually every night. We needed some wheels. We went to an auction with our brother Ed and bought a used Plymouth Voyager for $2,100. We wish we could tell you it was a cool hippie VW bus from the 1960s. Let's be honest: It was a burgundy soccer mom minivan, the only one there in our price range. It was definitely not going to help our game with women, but it proved to be dependable. And when we yanked out all the backseats, it became a mobile merchandising machine. It also acted as our motel, our office, and our warehouse. We called that van "The Enterprise," not only because we wanted to "boldly go where no T-shirt guys had gone before," but also because when we were in it, and our inventory was in it, and our cash was in it, that was the entire enterprise.

We took The Enterprise for extended six-week road trips traveling up and down the East Coast, hawking shirts door-to-door in every school from Maine to Virginia. Some nights were friendly and fruitful (thank you, UConn, Princeton, Bucknell). Other nights—most in fact—were filled with hundreds of rejections, ranging from "No, thank you," and "I like the shirt, but I don't have any money," to "Get the hell out of here!" Late nights were spent stretching the limits of any logical

Van go—on the road with The Enterprise in the early 1990s

sales curfew before circling around in the van for a spot dark enough to crash for the night on top of the shirts in the back.

Some dorms welcomed two random, bedraggled T-shirt salesmen, and others did not. (We happened to have been harmless, but campus security has rightfully been significantly beefed up since those days.) Some nights, a friendly resident assistant would give us "the soft boot": "I'm sorry, if you don't have a special permit, we can't let you solicit in the dorms." Other nights, we'd receive "the hard boot" from campus police who would escort us or chase us off university grounds. A few times, we were officially hauled in and banned from campus.

Being chased out of Pennsylvania's Gettysburg College by a campus cop with a megaphone riding in a golf cart that maxed out at six miles an hour remains a special moment for us ("Both of you: Drop your bags and stop!"). Being scatted off the University of New Hampshire campus at 3 a.m. and then out of town by a screaming, pitchfork-wielding farmer at 5 a.m. is equally funny now, but was not so funny then.

Looking back, we see these experiences prepared us well for the long haul of business ups and downs. We also see that although we can't change the past, we can decide on the focal points that will help us grow stronger. How we choose to frame a memory (crushing or comical) often determines the value and impact of that memory on our lives. We can choose frames that DIScourage or we can choose frames that ENcourage. The choice is ours.

Reflection on Rejection

We can choose how to frame our experiences, but we can't change the business results of those early years. We tried and failed a thousand times. We absorbed a lot of feedback accompanied by the word "no," forcing us to repeatedly adjust our game. Was the "no" due to the graphic, the price, our bad haircuts, or the fact that we were waking someone to pitch them a T-shirt at one in the morning? Or was the student simply out of cash? We jotted down and discussed the feedback every week, and adjusted our approach accordingly.

For example, we learned to visit the best dorms on mid-week nights instead of mopey Mondays or ghost town Friday nights. We learned about different campus cultures and about where different messages and designs resonated most.

Some people are afraid to try because they are afraid to fail. One helpful way to look at trying is this: There is no losing. That's right.

ALL SHIRTS DESIGNED BY THESE LANKY GENTLEMEN

Sign that was propped up in the street in the early 1990s

When you try, you either succeed or you learn. In both, you win. Finding minimal commercial success in those years, we listened and learned a lot. Alone, either one of us may have felt more discouraged or defeated by the "nos." Together, we were able to discuss and view each one as an opportunity.

Over time, you can become less fazed by rejection and setbacks if you recognize that each is taking you ultimately on a deeper, more fulfilling journey. In effect, you learn to answer "Yes, and" even to the "nos."

Whether in your personal or professional life, it takes courage to embrace the idea that rejection makes you stronger. And fear makes you braver. Fear is natural. It's never a matter of erasing fear completely. It's about acknowledging our fears but not being stopped by them, about working with and through them—one challenge at a time.

Soak It Up

Back in Boston, between road trips, we'd set up a card table at high-traffic times in the city's busiest neighborhoods, selling right from our duffel bags. One day in 1992, in the midst of a long sales dry spell, we were hawking shirts outside Boston's famous Faneuil Hall Marketplace when we felt a few raindrops splashing our arms. We started packing up all our freshly printed tees into a big cardboard box. Suddenly the skies opened up and we found ourselves in the middle of one of those Northeast downpours that erase all visibility. As we were wildly stuffing the T-shirts into the soaked cardboard box, it exploded into a sodden mess on the cobblestone sidewalk.

Our rationality drowned by the deluge, we kept frantically trying to repack the wet shirts into the now nonexistent box. Then we became aware of the sound of laughter from well-dressed tourists tucked under their umbrellas. As it swelled all around us, we quickly realized how pathetic we must have looked. Our peaking frustration, stress, and despair gave way to exhausted laughter. We shook our fists dramatically at the merciless skies, sat down in a growing puddle, and howled at our own ineptitude. A few people clapped, and then a few more, and finally the whole crowd started cheering and clapping. Drenched to the bone, the soaking wet T-shirts now just lying on the sidewalk, we stood up, opened our arms in mock triumph to our adoring fans, and took bows. Sometimes courage is admitting to yourself and others that you're licked—at least for the day.

Street hawking at a South Boston parade, 1993

Dealing With Doubt

From the start, we saw the T-shirt as a great vehicle for communication. What you say on the outside says a lot about who you are on the inside. We just needed to figure out what we wanted to say.

Our earliest attempts to design shirts were beautiful, *in our own*

minds, but they failed to connect. They included elaborate tribal patterns, eight-color prints, and ambiguous or nonexistent messages. They had no common thread. In response, our friends would say, "That's cool." Customers would say absolutely nothing (with voice or wallet).

We still loved traveling, writing, drawing, meeting people, and trying to build something—yet the numbers kept reminding us that our business was *barely* a business. From a financial standpoint, we were wildly unsuccessful. Meanwhile, we drifted into our late 20s. Occasionally, a friend would wonder aloud why we were still doing "that T-shirt thing." Bert was devastated when a girlfriend broke up with him. "He's almost 30 years old," her mother had told her, "and he still shares a van with his brother. You need to get real."

> One foot in, and one foot back. But it don't pay to live like that.
> —*The Avett Brothers*

Our friends were getting real jobs, buying grown-up clothes, cars, real homes, and even starting families. This naturally made us question our own life choices. Doubt cast a heavy shadow in those days. Doubt about the sustainability of actually doing what we loved. Doubt about how many soft boots, hard boots, and general rejections we could withstand. During many dark nights on the outskirts of an unwelcoming town, we contemplated where the road might end for The Enterprise.

What we know now is that if you choose to listen to the skeptics in your path, or let your natural self-doubts consume you, you'll take the safe route every time. In doing so, you'll pass up the chance to realize your potential. Lean on trusted friends to help you find the courage to overcome fear and doubt, and to persevere long enough to discover your opportunities.

FUEL:
COURAGE

Dear Life is Good,

When I was 16 years old, my father came to me and told me he had gotten test results that showed there was something seriously wrong with me, but we didn't know what. I grew up instantly in that moment. That is how I came to know that I have dermatomyositis, a rare autoimmune disease that affects my muscles. The disease affects only three people in a million, and 30 percent of cases are fatal. I still laugh at the fact that I had a better chance of winning the lottery. In order to heal my body of this degenerative disease, I had to weather three years of chemotherapy.

At one point during my recovery, when I was feeling the worst, my girlfriend at the time gave me a Life is Good hat. It was a little thing that ended up helping me through some brutal days. Every time I was pissed off at the world and wanted to call it quits, there was that three-word phrase staring back at me in the mirror. I couldn't argue with its simplicity. From that time on, I have tried to make it a point to take a LIG hat with me wherever I go. I have used it as a conversation piece to help others who are facing their own challenges. It always feels good to pass one along when I see somebody struggling.

This month is the ten-year anniversary of my diagnosis. I still have difficulties with my disease at times, but for the most part I am a healthy and happy 26-year-old. I was able to graduate college and now work with kids in a science museum in Milwaukee. To those who are unfamiliar with titanic obstacles, it may be difficult to understand how powerful such simple words can be. Those who have been in similar situations know it helps to have a guiding light. To me, Life is Good means so much. It gave me the extra boost that was needed to get over the hump. I'm here, I'm alive, I'm healthy. Life is good!

Dave Gahl

THREE WAYS TO BE COURAGEOUS

1. **JOIN THE TRY-ATHLON.** The one called life. It's up to you how many new things you're willing to try. People like Edison and the Wright brothers are extreme examples, but all of us have opportunities that beckon us. It takes courage to confront fear and uncertainty—to acknowledge them and try something new anyway. The start is the hardest part. Your biggest step into unknown territory is your very first one. You might pursue a new health initiative or hobby. Take on a tough project at work or at home, or try to improve a relationship with someone you love. The key word is "try." Yes, the work—the very act of trying—will teach you how to do it.

2. **SEE REJECTION AS YOUR BEST TEACHER.** And your coach and personal trainer. Instead of being defensive, try lowering your guard to actually take life's punches and learn from them. The people who care about you most may snub you to wake you out of a funk. A co-worker—or your whole family—may feed you some harsh, direct advice that's hard to swallow. You can choose to deny or counterpunch, or you can absorb some truths, and use them to adjust and grow stronger. Handling rejection is challenging, but it can also lead to the most profound and positive personal changes.

3. **LOOK FORWARD.** Challenges and adversity await us all. There will be moments of self-doubt, skeptics in our path, and external forces inviting us to focus on what's wrong with the world. Look to inspiring examples like our sister Berta and Dave Gahl to help guide you through the harder times. Acknowledge your setbacks, but train your mind to "put 'em in the rearview" and focus on your progress. That courageous choice enables you to get beyond obstacles and realize a world of opportunity.

FEAR.
LESS.

LICITY

Simplify.

Optimistic by Nature

Walden Pond is a beautiful swimming hole in Concord, Massachusetts, not too far from Boston. On the north end of the pond, a trail through the woods leads you to the original site of Henry David Thoreau's famous "tiny house"—a 10-by-15-foot cabin. He lived there for two years beginning in 1845, spending his time reading, writing, thinking, growing his own food, and making a few friends (yes, there were neighbors).

Thoreau removed extraneous stuff so that his mind could grow. "Our life is frittered away by detail," he wrote. "Simplify! Simplify!"

His friend and mentor, Ralph Waldo Emerson, busted his chops by noting that "One 'Simplify' would have sufficed." True, and funny—but Thoreau did have a point. And his point is even more relevant in today's digital age.

As the world around us grows increasingly complex, we crave simplicity more than ever. The rate of technological advancements in communications is startling. We now have constant access to an infinite sea of information. There are many positive aspects to all of this, but Thoreau had the foresight to see that there is also a flip side to such progress. "Men are becoming the tools of their tools," he observed. He was right. We all know there's a fine line in modern life between the gift of connectivity and the pitfalls of infomania. "I went to the woods because I wished to live deliberately," wrote Thoreau, "and see if I could learn what it had to teach, and not, when I came to die, discover that I had not lived."

We are not suggesting you pull up stakes and drop out of society completely. But we can all take inspiration from Thoreau's core principle of simplicity. There's a reason practices like meditation and yoga have become valuable to so many people today. We have a yearning to clear our minds while strengthening our bodies and spirits. Less is more when it comes to our daily schedules, our communication devices, the ingredients in our food, our choices for design, our architecture, and virtually every other aspect of our lives. Try sitting through a PowerPoint presentation riddled with bullets of tiny text, and then feel your shoulders relax and your mind open wide when the next slide on the screen is one simple, colorful image presented to illustrate one, smart point. Similarly, complex musical arrangements can awe and amaze us, but few things go straight to our hearts like a single, raw acoustic guitar.

Breaking News

By early fall of 1994, after five years on the road with our traveling T-shirt show, we had learned a lot and collected some good stories. But the prospects for our business were grim.

Cruising in The Enterprise from state to state had given the two of us the opportunity to discuss a broad range of topics. (Cell phones hadn't yet gone mainstream, so we had few interruptions.) On a long drive home from Philadelphia to Boston after a less-than-fruitful sales trip, a recurring and puzzling topic resurfaced. We were disturbed by the idea that, generally speaking, the news we received every day was (and sadly, still is today) overwhelmingly negative. You turn on the six o'clock news, and you really don't get the six o'clock news, do you? Instead, you get the six o'clock violent murder report. Bad things do happen. But you know what? Good things happen too. So where's the balance? Where's the good news? And what's the price we pay for the constant barrage of images and information about murders, fires, corruption, terrorism, and the threat of the next deadly epidemic?

think outside the box

In the eye-opening book *The Better Angels of Our Nature*, Steven Pinker provides an undeniable case that, despite common perception, violence has steadily declined worldwide since the beginning of civilization.

In our travels, we saw the impact of so much bad news first-hand. Students on campus with worried or horrified looks on their faces seemed always to be catching each other up on the latest sensational disasters. It was the same with people on the streets. Wherever we mixed with customers, it was clear that the negative news cycle had a significant effect on the way people felt and acted. Being optimists, we were really bothered by this. Pessimism is worse than counterproductive, we thought. It's corrosive. And we realized that the mass media play a big role in spreading pessimism.

But then—in the midst of our ugly discussion, right in the dark, gloomy center of it—we saw an opportunity. What if? What if instead of harping on what's wrong with the world, we could help people focus on what's right with the world? If we really want to find solutions, why not create a rallying cry for optimists?

Three Simple Words

By the end of that year, sales on the road weren't strong enough on their own to keep us in business. We had rented a cheap apartment back in Boston, which was doubling as a design space for custom jobs. Creating T-shirt graphics for gas stations, local bars, and softball teams wasn't our dream work, but it was helping to keep our dream alive. Sparsely furnished, the apartment was also an ideal spot for good old-fashioned keg parties, which our friends had come to expect whenever we returned from voyages in The Enterprise.

When we got back from one particular road trip, we weren't exactly in party mode, but we sucked it up and threw a good bash anyway. It was a ritual, and the parties were actually useful for our business. We'd supply the beer and a few tales from our travels, and in return our friends would give us feedback about new T-shirt designs that we taped up around the room. Instead of including blank paper for their feedback, we let them write what they wanted on the walls, right next to the drawings, which added to the fun.

A great crowd showed up for one memorable party. We were both enjoying the chance to catch up with friends, so we hadn't made time that night to look over the comments on the walls. When we got up in the morning, it was clear that one loose, simple sketch of a bohemian guy with a giant smile had stolen the show. There were dozens of notes around that drawing, and one of them jumped out at us. A girl at the party had drawn an arrow pointing to the face and wrote, "This guy's got life figured out." We thought that was pretty cool. We also thought it was pretty long, so we distilled it into three simple words: "Life is Good."

Street Cred

Two days after the party, we printed 48 "Life is Good" T-shirts for a street fair in Cambridge, Massachusetts. We laid the shirts out on our card table, like so many times before, and hoped for the best.

The original Jake and Life is Good sketch taped to a wall, 1994

Hunter
5 yrr

Life is good

Within a few minutes, a big dude with a Harley tattoo walked up to our table, smiled at the shirts, and bought an XL. Boom! Next was a chatty, young schoolteacher whose face lit up when she told us her latest goal was to make every hour in her class "happy hour." Those

John in Cambridge, Massachusetts, on the first day ever selling
Life is Good in September 1994

first two customers couldn't have been more different from each other, but they bought the same shirt. That was just the beginning. We sold the shirts to college students, policemen, waitresses, skateboarders, hippies, and businessmen. They were the easiest sales we ever had. People "got it," and they bought it. No explanation was necessary. The steady trickle became a frenzy, and in less than an hour, we were sold out. We had been selling T-shirts for five years. We had experienced good days and bad, but we had never seen anything like this. We sold 48 T-shirts in less than an hour. We literally sold the last two shirts off our backs. We were shocked, fired up, and scared to death all at the same time.

The simplicity of the message was magnetic to seemingly everyone who walked by. "Life is Good" said more with three words in one hour than all our elaborate pitches, messages, and designs had said in five years. It was the answer to our puzzle from so many conversations in The Enterprise. We had found our rallying cry for optimists, and those three simple words would change our lives forever.

> Simplicity is the ultimate sophistication.
> —*Leonardo da Vinci*

Brief Case

The lesson that first Life is Good T-shirt taught us about effective communication has stuck with us: Chisel away at the excess, and cut to the core. Say more with less. As Mark Twain once said, "If I had more time, I would have written a shorter letter." The same principle applies whenever you truly want to be heard—whether as a parent disciplining a stubborn child, an employee trying to influence a boss, or a friend sharing advice from the heart. Keep it simple.

In 1995, the first company mission statement we ever wrote for Life is Good was long and proud: "To have a greater positive impact on human culture than any clothing brand in history." Big and bold, we thought! The problem with it was twofold: First, no one remembered it. Second, it didn't welcome others to join us on the adventure. It only took about a decade for this reality to dawn on us. And what saved the day? Simplicity.

In 2004, we changed our company mission to one that people could easily remember and participate in: "To spread the power of optimism." It was so simple that it stuck, and we still love it today. Once we defined and communicated our mission, every other business decision became a lot easier. Does a new opportunity help us spread the power of optimism? If the answer is yes, we explore it. If the answer is no, we take a pass. Whether at work or in your personal life, defining the purpose of anything in the simplest terms possible makes it easier for you to land quickly on clear, definitive answers.

TEN SONGS OF SIMPLICITY

- "Gone" Jack Johnson
- "Imagine" John Lennon
- "Country Pie" Bob Dylan
- "I'd Like To" Corinne Bailey Rae
- "Homegrown" Zac Brown Band
- "Slow Down" Jesse Dee
- "Old Old Fashioned" Frightened Rabbit
- "Blue, Red and Grey" The Who
- "Diner" Martin Sexton
- "We're Going to Be Friends" The White Stripes

Five hundred years ago, da Vinci said, "Simplicity is the ultimate sophistication." That's never been more true than today. As the world gets more and more complex, the happiest and most productive people in it find ways to simplify.

In business, if you bring a complex idea to market, you'll reach hundreds. Simplify it and you'll reach thousands. Simplify it to the point where the average person instantly understands it, and your reach becomes limitless.

Real It In

If we take a real wide view, we can see technology bettering our lives at a rapid pace. We're entering an era in which technological innovation will play a central role in raising the standard of living for every person on this planet. That's important for us to point out—in general, we're pro-technology. However, we also recognize that the access to and constant availability of powerful technological tools presents a real threat to our peace of mind, physical health, and overall well-being.

Recommended Reading: In *Abundance: The Future Is Better Than You Think,* Peter Diamandis (founder of XPRIZE) and Steven Kotler make a compelling case that technology and scientific innovation are making the world a safer, healthier, and happier place for all.

Slow down everyone. You're moving too fast. —*Jack Johnson*

It's strange how many of us choose to stuff our lives with busyness and distractions. When we're *too* busy, we don't do anything well. Our relationships suffer, our performance at work suffers, and we don't enjoy our lives. Yet being "crazy busy" is a badge of honor for some people.

As hyperconnected digital warriors of the 21st century, we take pride in somehow keeping pace with the daily race. The adrenaline rush of speeding through many tasks and communications in a day can be addictive. It can reinforce an illusion that we are always in high demand—and moving toward something grand. This frantic cycle is generally not good for our health, our productivity, or our happiness. And if it goes unchecked, it can lead any of us to burnout and depression.

How can we reclaim our lives? How can we slow down, regain our handle, and focus on the things that matter most: time with our favorite people, fulfilling projects, activities or hobbies that bring us joy?

In short, the power of simplicity is in our selectivity: cutting down and weeding out the extraneous "stuff" (we all have it) in order to focus our time and energy on the people we love and the things we love to do.

Less Is More

One very effective move for us has been to severely reduce the volume of digital communication we're required to digest to run our business. A few years back we were feeling increasingly like the men Thoreau described: We were becoming the tools of our tools. The time we spent daily just shoveling out our email inboxes was daunting. And we were going to bed at night feeling guilty and inadequate because we couldn't get ahead. The more emails we sent out, the more flowed back in. Sound familiar?

The answer for us was a radical one. We dropped our email accounts entirely. Just disappeared—no more email. We walked out the door onto the street, and we were free men. We kept wondering if people were going to get upset, or if the email police would come to arrest us, but they never did.

Our own productivity rose. Our contacts made quick, healthy adjustments. Our sharp and diligent team at Life is Good began prioritizing only the most important communications and summarizing with us every two weeks. Liberating, and far more efficient. It's been a few years now, and we have never missed email for a minute.

Most people don't think they can survive without email, but many can. What happens is that you are simply more selective about giving out your contact information. Before you say you could never do this, or you could never drop off of Facebook or any other time-consuming social media, consider this question: What do you give it, and what does it give back to you?

Unplug.

Feed the Good Wolf

We can all take a hard look at separating the inessentials from the essentials in our lives. Maybe you're a news or social media junkie who will find that the world doesn't stop—and that you CAN survive—without your reading the news every morning, watching it every evening, or checking your Facebook account a dozen times a day. You don't have to go cold turkey, but recognize that setting limits and choosing your sources wisely can help elevate you above the noise.

FIVE INSPIRING SITES TO FEED YOUR GOOD WOLF

- soulpancake.com
- positivelypositive.com
- tinybuddha.com
- huffingtonpost.com/good-news
- lifeisgood.com (positively shameless, we know)

Discernment is a powerful skill to learn and to teach our kids. Is the communication we're digesting (via TV, social media, email, and so on) helping, inspiring, and enriching our lives? Or is it stoking our fears and negatively distorting our worldview and disposition? It's like the Cherokee parable of the old chief who tells his grandson about the two wolves (one good and one evil) that are fighting inside of every person, every day. After thinking about it, the boy asks, "Which wolf will win?" The chief replies, "The one you feed."

Is it possible for you to feed your Good Wolf more vittles? Sure, by living with intention. We're not coaching you off the grid entirely. It's all about selectivity. Maybe you limit yourself to one or two Facebook check-ins a day. Set an example for your kids by limiting your own daily screen time and by choosing content that inspires rather than deflates you. Switch your phone to vibrate and tuck it away during meals. Have a favorite show or two? Love to watch movies? Great. Choose, savor, and enjoy those tune-in times consciously, and then take a pass on the roving remote and its sea of infinite pixels constantly clamoring for your attention.

People often say they can't "find the time" to do what they love. It takes a conscious effort to *make* the time by simplifying, cutting away the negative distractions, and feeding your Good Wolf.

Peace Out

Thoreau figured out the recipe so long ago: Reduce the amount of stuff in our lives in order to think more clearly, live more fully, and enjoy the beauty that surrounds us more deeply. He chose to make his passionate plea for simplicity while living in the woods with good reason.

The pull of the great outdoors is as much about what's *not* out there as about what is. When we're able to get outside to explore the trails and the trees, take a dive into the ocean, or come up for air in the mountains, our bodies and our minds say, "Thank you." Yes, there's gratitude for the palpable beauty of autumn leaves, crashing waves, or spectacular peaks rising above the tree line. But our senses may be most grateful for the release—from the gripping intensity and fractured focus of our modern lives.

Fresh air and a bit of unmarked time can do us all wonders. Imagine uninterrupted time: you and the people you love outside, just talking, roaming, playing. Physical clutter, mental clutter: gone. That's what nature can do for us all.

Your personal connection to nature might be found in nearby woods, a lake, your own backyard, or a public park in the city. A single favorite tree to lean on can do the trick. Recognize how healthy and necessary it is to ditch the modern world's frantic pace and complexity on occasion. Mother Nature is always at the ready to help clear your noggin and refresh your senses.

FUEL:
SIMPLICITY

Dear Jacobs brothers,

Several years ago, I began working at Eastern Mountain Sports in Tonawanda, New York. The first employee purchase I made was my Life is Good shirt with the simple message "Get Out" in the color Sky. That shirt went with me on every camping trip, every kayak or canoe excursion, and on more than one occasion when I was snowshoeing to classes. Once I graduated from college, I began a graduate degree in humanities. This current academic semester is my final one and it is an internship in Los Angeles (very far from my native New England). I packed my car with all the essentials for life in L.A.: Frisbees, snowshoes, all my camping gear, books, sewing machine, and a decade worth of journals and diaries.

En route to my new but temporary digs in L.A., my car was robbed and almost everything was taken. As traumatic as this experience was, I was happy to realize that my LIG shirt, the most comfortable and uplifting article of clothing I own, was with me in the hotel room. I was wearing it, in fact. And for the following 74 hours this shirt was one of three items I had left to my name (the other two were my car, thankfully, and a quilt I had made). I love that shirt more every day for reminding me what really matters. Thank you for keeping me going. And if you ever need a short story or a quilt or a snowshoeing partner, please let me know.

Life rocks,
Erica B. Davis

THREE WAYS TO SIMPLIFY YOUR LIFE

1. **MATTER UP!** Decide what and who is most important in your life, and say yes to them. Say no to everything else. "Yes" is one of the most powerful words in any language, but "no" can be equally helpful when applied to extraneous clutter: physical stuff, calendar fillers, and general infomania. Clothes you haven't worn or toys your kids haven't played with in over a year? Give 'em away. (Hold on to the ball and the big box—those toys never get old.) Social obligations that drain more than they fuel your positive energy? Politely take a pass.

2. **UNPLUG.** Aggressively cut down your media consumption, screen time, emails, and meetings with people who light up a room *when they leave it.* Pull back from the negative news cycle, choosing to get what you need in brief from a reliable source. Set specific limits for yourself on times and frequency of digital communication. Try to unplug a good hour or two before bedtime. Digital screens, including smartphones, make falling asleep harder and lead to less restful slumber. Make some of these adjustments and you'll instantly see the benefits. You'll find you have more clarity—and more time for the people, projects, and hobbies you love.

3. **TAKE IT OUTSIDE.** Sexy ads and short-lived fads will always peddle nonsense as substance and keep some people on the hamster wheel chasing external status symbols. For most of us, the things that actually make us happy are the same things we loved as children: fresh air, laughter, and playing with family and friends. Get outside to breathe, clear your mind, and enjoy those simple pleasures. And while you're not keeping up with the Joneses, they'll be jonesing for what you have: a life of true depth, joy, and meaning.

TAKE IT

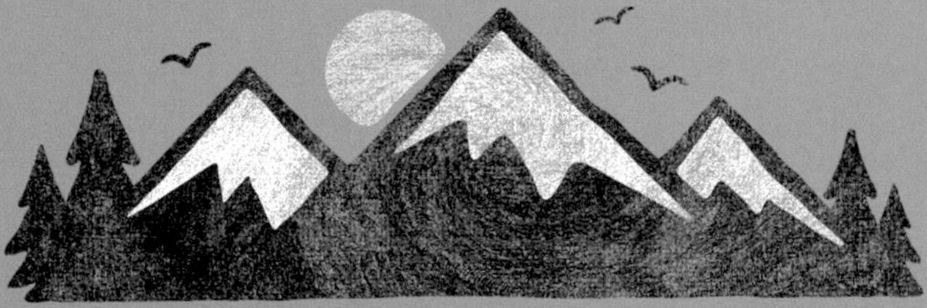

OUTSIDE

Create Your Own Happy Hour

The same month and year that we sold the first Life is Good T-shirts in the street—September 1994—Ken Burns debuted an 18.5-hour documentary series called *Baseball*. With his signature montage of archival photos, period music, classic film footage, and interviews, it was an artistic look at the great American pastime. As lifelong baseball fans, we made it our business to record and watch every episode together. And as it turns out, we weren't the only ones watching. This masterpiece of storytelling had 45 million viewers, which made it the most watched program in public television history.

The series profiled the greatest players ever to take the field, including Babe Ruth, Joe DiMaggio, and Willie Mays. Yet the player we walked away talking about the most was a great power hitter from the late 1920s and early '30s named "Hack" Wilson. Why? Because we couldn't stop laughing at the line Burns borrowed from an old sportswriter to describe him: "He was built along the lines of a beer keg, and not unfamiliar with its contents." That hilarious description was our number one takeaway. We must have repeated it and laughed about it a hundred times. As we write this book, it's two decades later, and we still reference Hack on occasion, just to share a laugh with friends.

We all love to laugh. It just feels good. And we always remember the funny things, because we want to laugh again. Laughter is also the great connector. We love to share laughs with friends, old and new. Humor is, in fact, the best social lubricant there is. It breaks down social barriers fast and brings us together.

Company-wide "Jake Jams" combine good laughs with business updates.

Humor also happens to be seriously good for you. Laughter has therapeutic value and promotes overall health and wellness. When we laugh, it actually changes our body chemistry in very positive ways. Laughing regularly reduces stress and anxiety, releases muscle tension, boosts our energy, lowers our blood pressure, improves overall cardiac health, triggers the release of endorphins and dopamine (our natural happiness transmitters), strengthens our immune system, and helps us sleep better. Now that's a superpower!

Laughter is more infectious than the common cold, and a lot more fun. So go ahead: Start laughing more, and get your friends and family laughing more too. You'll all enjoy the ride, and you're likely to live longer too. With all these medical and therapeutic benefits, maybe laughter really is the best medicine—especially when we take into account that it's free.

TEN ALL-TIME NOT-TO-BE-MISSED COMEDIES

- *Anchorman*
- *Best in Show*
- *Bridesmaids*
- *Superbad*
- *The Big Lebowski*
- *There's Something About Mary*
- *Beautiful Girls*
- *Monty Python and the Holy Grail*
- *Old School*
- *Rushmore*

Good Vibes Are Contagious

After we sold out of those first 48 LIG shirts in the street, we knew we had something special. We just had no idea what to do with it. So we did what any red-blooded Bostonians do when they're puzzling over something. We drove down to Cape Cod, went for a swim in the sea (it's free you know, just like laughter), and hoped Mother

Ocean would give us the answer. And you know what? She did! It wasn't exactly a stroke of genius, so let's call it a stroke of common sense. (Strokes of genius, by the way, are rare, and in most cases, high maintenance. Strokes of common sense, on the other hand, get the job done just fine, and are far easier to execute.) Remember now, we weren't a couple of Al Gores trying to invent the "interweb"—we were just trying to jump-start a T-shirt business.

Our stroke of common sense was that we should try to sell these Life is Good shirts by the dozens to retailers. We had talked about this before, but until now we really didn't have a design we thought was worthy. We jumped into The Enterprise in our soaking wet board shorts and appointed each other the leaders of the new Life is Good wholesale department. "Congratulations!" "Why thank you, and same to you, sir!"

As we toted around our one Life is Good design, here are a couple of the open-minded and downright brilliant responses we got: "What does Life is Good mean?" and "Life is Good? What's so good about it?" Thank you! Have a good day. Thank you very much. We took turns trying new pitches, and the rejections might have dragged us down. But each time we got back in the van, one of us would imitate the rejections, and pretty soon we were cracking each other up. Our favorite came from a mountain of a man with a long, crazy beard who looked over the shirts very slowly and carefully, and then advised us like we were his own brothers: "If these are stolen, you guys managed to steal some stupid shit."

Humor is most potent when morale is low. One funny line, funny face, or crazy imitation can raise the spirits. It can also break the tension, reset the table, and refocus people on opportunities.

As the sun was going down on old Cape Cod, our day was saved by one courageous optimist in a small flip-flop shop. With a weathered

Red Sox cap on her head and a delightful smile on her face, our new friend Nancy bought two dozen shirts. "I love it!" she said. "Let's give it a try . . . By the way, what's the smiley guy's name?"

We decided to call our man Jake, short for Jacobs. Only much later did we learn that "jake" is also an old-fashioned expression that means "Everything's all right" or "Everything's cool."

Two weeks later, Nancy remained our only wholesale account. Doing what we could to pay the rent, we were working on a custom T-shirt design for a local landscaping company when the phone rang. It was Nancy. She had sold all 24 units of the Life is Good T-shirt and was looking for more. Great news! She also had an interesting question: "Our store is next to an ice cream shop, remember? Well my husband and I were talking. We think life is pretty good when you're having an ice cream." We were a little slow on the uptake and had no idea where she was going. "So we were wondering," she continued, "does Jake eat ice cream?" Now we got it. "No," we said, "but he will!" As we braced ourselves, we could hear Nancy and her husband laughing their heads off on the other end. To be honest, the response wasn't even meant to be funny, but we ended up joining in on the laughter.

Humor puts us on common ground. When we laugh together, we connect quickly. And humor builds trust. Nothing accelerates relationship building like the bridge of humor. After that phone call, Nancy was on our team. She was on a mission to spread good vibes with us.

We sketched a new Jake right away, placing a delicious ice cream cone in his hand. Voilà! Within two days, we printed and shipped the Life is Good ice cream shirts, and the reports came back quickly that they were outselling the original design. Thank you, Nancy.

You might think we would have figured out on our own where this comedy act was going next, but we didn't. The next call came

from Nancy's sister-in-law, who lived in Vermont. "Nancy told me these Life is Good shirts are now her best sellers. We have a sporting goods store on a bike path, and we might like to try some. Does Jake ride a mountain bike?" This time our answer was a little bit smarter, "No, but he will . . . if you pay in advance." Again came the roaring laughter on the other end, and again we joined in. The prepaying part might have sounded like a joke, but it wasn't. We didn't have the money to stock inventory, so when she complied with the payment, Jake learned to ride a bike. Now we could see where this was going.

Word started spreading that optimism was selling. As Jake learned to hike and fish and play guitar, our customer base grew. We realized that all we had to do now was listen closely to what people truly loved to do, and then celebrate those things on T-shirts. Because our own dream jobs were unfolding right before our eyes, and because we wanted to encourage more people to spend their time doing the things they loved, we added the tagline "Do What You Love. Love What You Do." And it stuck.

As Christmas approached, our phone rang more and more. That year we sold $87,000 worth of Life is Good T-shirts at wholesale. Things were far from perfect with our business, but we kept stress down and spirits high by finding things to laugh about every day. And although we were making our share of operational mistakes, more often, we were making friends.

Pass the Ragú!

As the spring of 1995 rolled around, we had no sales force and no marketing campaign. But demand was growing just the same, and a steady stream of small orders was building. It became clear that we needed more hands on deck to manage the business, so we recruited Kerrie Gross, the adorable 23-year-old who had recently moved into the apartment upstairs from us. We had instant chemistry with her, and she had already started volunteering her time by night to help us organize the business. So we decided to offer her a full-time position. Instead of telling her how much the job paid or asking what her range was, the question we smoothly asked over dinner one night was, "What is the very least amount of money you could possibly get paid right now in order to pay your bills?" We were deadly serious, but we all laughed hysterically at the way it came out. After a few quick calculations, and as a foreshadowing of the "team-first" attitude that would make Kerrie an irreplaceable asset to LIG, she answered $17,000. She was hired immediately. She was given no job description, but we spent considerable time determining her title: "Business Manager," it was decided. Vague, yet official sounding. Perfect!

TEN FUNNY SONGS

- "A Boy Named Sue" Johnny Cash
- "Mahna Mahna" The Muppets
- "Handy Man" Animal Liberation Orchestra
- "Bob Dylan's 115th Dream" Bob Dylan
- "A Comedian at the Oscars" Will Ferrell, Jack Black, John C. Reilly
- "King Tut" Steve Martin
- "Red Hooded Sweatshirt" Adam Sandler
- "Lazy Sunday" The Lonely Island
- "Freeker by the Speaker" Keller Williams
- "Business Time" Flight of the Conchords

On her first day, Kerrie made the outlandish suggestion that we invest in a computer, a fax machine, and a business telephone system that would connect our apartments. "Whoa! Whoa, young lady! Where do you think you are, IBM?!" We reluctantly agreed to the first two items, but we put our foot down on the third. The next day

we drilled a hole in Kerrie's floor and dropped some wires through. "Now we are connected!" And the hole came in handy to yell up or down when it was time for lunch.

We got lucky with our brilliant recruitment of the girl upstairs. Kerrie turned out to be smart, resourceful, and fiercely loyal. And she rarely finished all the food on her plate, which also came in handy for us. The year we hired her, 1995, we did $262,000 in top-line sales. And we celebrated like we just won the World Series, because we had managed to pay our first employee, and stay in business. It was a big step.

In early 1996, we still had no warehouse, so boxes were piling up in our kitchen. Customers called to reorder shirts and we would literally say, "Let me check the inventory in the kitchen." They always laughed when we said that, so we started to play it up and share things like what we had in the fridge—usually appetizing combinations like pickles and expired milk.

That same year we got our first test with a national retailer, a chain out of Indianapolis called Galyan's that was widely considered the best sporting goods retailer in the country. (It was later acquired by Dick's Sporting Goods, which remains a great customer today.) When the test was successful, their executives invited us to fly to Indianapolis for a meeting about next steps. This was huge, but there was a problem. We were so tight on cash, we couldn't afford the airfare. So we fessed up, and put an interesting plan together. They were coming to Boston to spend a day with the people at Reebok in about a month. Their meetings were scheduled to finish by 5 p.m., and Reebok had provided them with a car to go

Kerrie Gross working a street fair in Cambridge, Massachusetts, in the mid-1990s

wherever they wanted after that. "That's great," we said. "Why don't you ask the driver to take you to our apartment for dinner?" We didn't let on that our entire business was at our apartment. When that night came, three top executives sat down and ate with us in our little kitchen, which was overflowing with T-shirt boxes. It was Wednesday night, so we prepared our specialty for the occasion—Prince spaghetti from a box with Ragú sauce from a jar.

Our guests walked through the door with worn-out looks on their faces. Retail, like many industries, can be stressful. They must have had a long day, but they sure lightened up and had some fun as the night moved on. We really didn't talk much business at all, but we laughed our heads off. They made fun of our apartment and all the boxes, and we made fun of Indianapolis. At one point we went around the table boasting about our washed-up sports careers. When it was Kerrie's turn, she ran upstairs to fetch her pathetically small "Most Hustle" softball trophy—the one they always give to players who can't

hit, catch, or throw. The trophy was literally three inches tall. That got the biggest laugh of the night. The Galyan's crew was laughing so hard the spaghetti was coming out of their noses.

Laughter is a natural mechanism for releasing pent-up stress, tension, and anxiety. Life is too short to carry that weight around. Humor can lighten us up, and make us feel young and strong again. Before our guests arrived that night, we were nervous about our ability to entertain them. We needed the business from Galyan's, and we were worried about what they might think of us. As the evening wound down and it was time for them to go, the VP of Merchandising, Chris Campbell, stood up and said something we'll always cherish. "Tonight was humanizing. I haven't laughed like that in a long time. Business sometimes treats us like machines, but machines don't laugh like we did tonight. Thank you." Special words to remember from a special night. Over the next few years, Galyan's would become our biggest account—the one that took the Life is Good brand national.

FUEL:
HUMOR

Dear Bert and John,

I have had a Life is Good hat for many years now. It has been on my head almost the same amount of time. It has many holes and tears, the color is faded, and it has been with me through the best of times and the worst of times. My Life is Good hat has been wet, dry, buried, frozen, sunbaked, shot, painted, taped, on fire, kicked, stolen, rescued, muddy, lost, found, used as a Frisbee, traveled to 19 states, blew off my head at the Grand Canyon, been dragged along on eight whitewater rafting trips, countless backpacking trips, and thousands of campouts, seen better days at Put-in-Bay, helped save a beer in Lake Erie, been in my back pocket for thousands of miles riding on the bike, fielded a ground ball, been the only piece of clothing worn skinny-dipping (bear watching), was run through the dishwasher and a car wash, was run over by a semitruck, chewed by a dog, helped scare away a snake, swatted and killed a billion flies, held all kinds of salamanders, got dropped in a Porta-John, successfully stayed on my head through a kayak roll, has a hidden four leaf clover inside, has waved many a racer across the finish line, and it makes one hell of a great sun blocker while lying in my hammock.

My LIG hat is just like me, weathered and well tested, but still in the game!

**Sincerely,
Doug Smathers**

Let's face it: It's hard not to like Doug. We all appreciate people who can make us laugh, and we're drawn to those who laugh more freely. We're especially drawn to those who are able to laugh at themselves. That takes a special confidence.

Light 'Em Up

By the summer of 1996, it was clear that the size of our little business would more than double again. We were still too scared to take on the rent of a real warehouse, but we had outgrown the kitchen, so we found a happy medium. Midland Graphics in Marlborough, Massachusetts, was our main T-shirt supplier and screen printer. We asked the owners, Jim and Mike McCarthy, to let us park a 40-foot shipping container on the dirt lot next to their building in exchange for our small but growing print runs. They gave us the green light. Once we added shelving and inventory to form the makeshift warehouse, we realized it was pretty dark inside, so they also let us run electricity out from their print shop. Whew! Thanks, Jim and Mike.

> No sense being pessimistic. It wouldn't work anyway.
> —*Unknown*

During this time, we sent invoices out to our customers with the photo opposite and the message "Please pay on time so we can keep these lights on and pay our hungry warehouse staff." Our customers must have either appreciated the humor or just pitied us. We'll never know, but they paid their bills on time.

Humor, in general, is underutilized in business. It can truly give you a point of difference and a competitive advantage, especially where it's least expected. Several years later, we met a woman at a trade show who ran accounts payable for one of our customers. She told us she paid our bills first every time because, in eight years on the job, ours was the only funny invoice she ever got.

Bring It On

In 1997, we added three more full-time employees and we broke $1 million in sales for the first time. We also moved into a real office and warehouse space in our hometown of Needham, Massachusetts. As we grew, we did our best to build an environment

Bert and John in the Life is Good "warehouse" in 1997

where our team felt comfortable laughing together as often as possible. When the leaders in an organization demand to be taken more seriously, their co-workers have a tendency to take them less seriously. The laughs will still take place, but they

This signage might be an HR violation today, but back then anything to make the crew laugh was welcome—including frequent pong tourneys in the new warehouse digs.

take place secretly behind closed doors, and they divide rather than unite.

Humor can be a great equalizer. When management is willing to let their guard down and laugh openly, especially at themselves, it invites others to do the same, and creates a happier, less intimidating space. Humor leads to more unity *and* productivity in the workplace. Because laughter relaxes us, it enables us to think more clearly as well as communicate and solve problems more effectively. It takes a conscious effort to bring humor to work every day, but the benefits to you and your teammates are limitless.

Funny Is Money

Every year, come April Fools' Day, we welcome the opportunity to give our customers a good laugh. The following was advertised as an actual product for sale on the Life is Good website . . .

> * *LIG Peanut Butter & Jelly Cologne:*
> *"The sweet smell of optimism is in the air."*

A little nonsense always drives serious traffic to our site. In fact, this April Fools' prank that included other absurd products broke our all-time record for visitors in a day, including all previous holidays. And while customers were having a laugh, they stuck around to buy real products and drive robust sales numbers too. What does that tell us? Humor's good for people, and it's also good for business.

Full disclosure: More than a few people actually got upset they couldn't buy the PB and J cologne. Life is Good just doesn't make scents. (We know, we know: terrible.)

THREE WAYS TO KEEP ON THE FUNNY SIDE

1. **BRING IT HOME.** Bring some laughter home to the people you love. Of course you might have any number of important matters to address with them, but first give five minutes to connect and lift the mood with something funny. Trust us, the serious stuff will go much better if you do. And kids thrive on silly, so if you have little ones around, shake off the furrowed brow (or just turn it into a gorilla or robot face) before you reengage at day's end. Rhyming, singing, or just making up outlandish proclamations is highly encouraged. "All baths shall be taken in either mustard, relish, or dragon brains tonight!"

2. **WORK IT AROUND.** Make it a point to enter work meetings, especially on Mondays, looking to infuse some laughter. You don't have to be Will Ferrell. Just share a personal anecdote—something you saw or read that made you laugh. Could be calling out your own ineptitude in some area. It's about connecting as humans before we connect as teammates. As Ron Burgundy says in *Anchorman,* "For just one night, let's not be co-workers. Let's be co-people." Teams that laugh together build greater unity and trust. And teams with greater unity and trust perform better. Laugh together and your office will be more enjoyable and more productive.

3. **GET YOUR VITAMIN L.** When most people think about health, they focus on nutrition and exercise. Don't forget about laughter. It may just be your quickest and most enjoyable way to positively impact your health. Take care of yourself by tapping your favorite sources for a good laugh often—from your favorite writer, filmmaker, comedian, site, or show, to your craziest co-worker or funniest friend. You'll find your strength and energy grows when your laughter flows.

WATCH OUT
FOR INVISIBLE
THINGS

 Life is good.

SUPERPOWER #5

GRATI

TUDE

FUEL:
GRATITUDE

Dear Bert and John,

My name is Alex. I have a brother Nick and we are ten. We both have extra challenges in the world, but at the end of the day we still have each other.

When I was born I had to have my leg amputated. Nick is blind. We were both born early and weighed a pound, so we had a lot of work to grow and get better.

Me and Nicky have all of your shirts with the things we like doing best. But if you ask us what we do best— and what makes us happy and laugh most—it's just being together. I know now that Nick has more challenges than I do, but he says and does things that make me laugh and forget feeling bad. I don't know how to describe it other than I love him.

You're lucky to have a brother too. I hope you do fun things together!

Your friends, Alex and Nick

Buddha at Ten

Several years ago, an incredible gift dropped on our desk: the letter above, containing the amazing insights of a ten-year-old with the wisdom of Buddha and the simple delivery of the kid next door. We were floored. It remains not only one of the most memorable letters we have ever received, but also one of the most powerful pieces of communication we have come across anywhere. Reading it again, our jaws just drop. How could one kid get so many things so right in so few words?

Alex's letter embodies many essential elements of the super-power gratitude. *"We both have extra challenges in the world—but at the end of the day we still have each other."* There's no more eloquent way to say it, and our sage at an early age captures many lessons in that single sentence alone. Maybe the most important lesson is the reminder that gratitude is not just a matter of thanking our lucky stars when our dreams come true; it's also about thankfulness right in the midst of our inevitable daily struggles.

Alex knows he and his brother have had "extra" challenges in their young lives. As we've learned over and over, it's the people who face the greatest challenges that gain an elevated sense of gratitude for life. They earn a heightened appreciation for everything around them, taking nothing for granted. It's a perspective that can serve us all. Alex takes nothing for granted, and his letter doesn't ask for anything. Instead, he chooses to celebrate what he has.

It helps to see gratitude as a choice. We get better at this super-power and absorb its many benefits when we make it a daily practice. Taking stock of the many people, experiences, and things that are good, right, and working well in our lives has an uncanny way of attracting more good. What we focus on grows.

Kids are generally pretty good at staying in the present: in the drawing, in the bathtub, in the sand castle of their little moments. As adults, we often let distractions fracture our moments. And we spend precious hours dwelling on the past or projecting too far into our future.

Focusing on the simple pleasures—on the good we are experiencing here, now, today—can do wonders. Otherwise, we can find ourselves defining happiness in terms of *someday:* "I'll be happy and grateful when I [fill in the blank]: ace that exam, land that big promotion, buy a new car, move into a new home, or meet that special someone." *Then*, I'll feel happy, grateful, and fulfilled. Someday, as the saying goes, is not a day of the week. And although these life milestones are worthy of celebration, they are no substitute for a foundation of gratitude that leads us to far more consistent happiness.

> Enjoy every
> sandwich.
> —*Warren Zevon*

It's all about our disposition. It's easy to look at the news and think the world is getting worse by the day. Gifted science writer Matt Ridley provides historical data to the contrary. His 2010 book *The Rational Optimist* acknowledges the world is far from perfect, but delivers hard evidence that life is getting better for almost all of humanity.

By elevating our awareness of what's right with the world, instead of focusing on what's wrong, we come to realize that the keys to happiness are all around us.

Like most brothers, we can square off occasionally on any topic, disagreeing in or outside of work. Before we know it, we might regress into juvenile one-upmanship. Then along comes someone

Consider yourself a
lucky dog.

like Alex to remind us we have a choice. Rather than taking each other for granted, we can shake it off and access gratitude any time: *"You're lucky to have a brother too."*

Fuel

Although Alex's letter is one of a kind, over the years we've received thousands of communications from people all over the world that have touched and inspired us. We share a number of them throughout this book. Those who write to us often find an authentic, personal connection to Life is Good's messages. We learned early on that this brand is not about us; it's about a broad community of optimists from all walks of life.

Customers have told us about wearing their LIG gear through major life events—the joys of weddings, births, adoptions, and reunions. And of course, while enjoying simple pleasures like hiking, grilling, camping, gardening, hanging with friends, or walking the dog. Even more often, people have been moved to share their stories of wearing Life is Good while holding tenaciously to their optimism through the toughest of times. Through the perils of joblessness, homelessness, the deaths of loved ones, chemotherapy, addiction, harrowing accidents, house fires, natural disasters, terrorist attacks, and more.

Over and over, people have told us that when they want to prepare themselves for a challenging day, or simply celebrate another one, they find in Life is Good a mantra that grounds them. We get some letters about our artwork or the softness of our T-shirts, but what matters to most people are the messages. For many, their clothing choice is both a self-reminder, as well as an empowering message for others. We have heard the same sentiment many times from cancer patients who wear our hats, and once from an amputee who tattooed Life is Good on his prosthetic: "I want others to see clearly that my attitude defines me, not my physical condition or life situation."

Eleven-year-old Lindsey Beggan provided big inspiration with her positive outlook despite being diagnosed with terminal bone cancer in 1998. Lindsey beat the cancer, and we're grateful to call the whole Beggan family friends to this day.

We didn't know what to do with these letters and emails when we first started receiving them. We were trying to figure out our little business, so while we read them and were moved by them, we just tucked them away in a drawer. We were busy discovering answers to basic questions like "What's a sales forecast?" But you can't keep something that good in a drawer. Around 2000, it finally dawned on us that all we had to do with these letters was *share* them. We started by sharing them internally with our own crew, reading them aloud before meetings and work shifts, and at company-wide gatherings. Back then, we were only a few dozen people. Today, the team of around 200 packs in and listens just as closely to every word. When the daily grind of activities begins to obscure the value of our work, these inspiring stories lift us up and remind us we are members of a much bigger tribe. That's why we gave this amazing flow of correspondence the name "Fuel." The ongoing journey of Life is Good is a road trip, and these letters and emails always refill our tank and recharge our spirits for the road ahead.

After a while we put a bound selection of Fuel letters in stores for our customers to discover, and posted a growing number of them on our website. Inspired sharing led to further inspired sharing, as a growing community of readers took the time to pass along their own stories. Looking back, we see how these riveting personal narratives from total strangers helped to shape our organization's singular, unifying mission: "To spread the power of optimism." Lesson learned yet again: Listen to your customers. Listen to the people around you. They will help you discover and express your best self.

Michael Franti, poet, composer, social justice activist, lead singer of Michael Franti & Spearhead, unstoppable optimist, and valued friend, has rocked out at several Life is Good events. Given up for adoption at birth, he has overcome obstacles to devote his adult life to spreading positive, empowering messages. His generosity of spirit is a product of his practiced gratitude and a reminder that what we focus on grows. He shared these thoughts at a recent fundraiser for The Life is Good Playmakers:

> It's hard to be grateful all the time, you know? And some days I wake up and I feel like I'm on the wrong side of the bed and I can't appreciate everything that happens around me. But I believe in practicing gratitude in the same way that you practice free throws, or anything else.

You can consciously choose to focus on what you're thankful for, rather than what frustrates you. And if you have positive thoughts, positive words, a positive mental attitude, and positive actions, then eventually it becomes easier and easier to be positive.

"Get To"

Fuel brought us something else we're grateful for: two simple words that can change our daily approach to many situations. They came to us by way of a letter from Regina Brett, an inspiring columnist for the *Cleveland Plain Dealer*. She wrote to us about her column entitled "Chemo Hat's Power Lies in the Message." It told the story of a time when life didn't feel good for her—when she was about to undergo her first chemotherapy treatment and couldn't imagine going bald. Her friend Frank

Michael Franti thanks a fan at a Life is Good Festival.

gave her a Life is Good baseball cap; she chronicled how she wore it until her hair grew back, and how it was subsequently passed along and worn by at least eight others who were undergoing chemo treatments.

So Frank's gift keeps rippling. But he had another gift. Here's how Regina described it:

> Frank is a magical kind of guy. A painter by trade, he lives by two simple words: Get to. They remind him to be grateful for everything. Instead of saying, "I have to go to work today," Frank tells himself, "I get to go to work." Instead of saying, "I have to get groceries," he gets to. It works for everything.

Simple phrases are powerful, and Frank's succinct nugget really spoke to us at Life is Good. In its simplicity and wisdom, it has become the Swiss army knife of gratitude. We have always believed that where others see obstacles, optimists see opportunities. Where some may feel burdened by daily tasks and commitments ("have tos"), it's possible for you to flick that mental light switch and turn them into "get tos." The choice is ours. "I *have to* write that report/do the laundry/pay the bills/pick up groceries." Or "I *get to* write that report/pay the bills," and so on. Most of us *get to* do these things because we have fingers to type, or a home to live in. We *get to* pick up the groceries because we have two legs to walk on, and two eyes to read the labels in the aisles, and live in a country with an incredible abundance of available food. That one little word choice (from *have* to *get*) represents a major mind shift that can help transform us from default pessimists to proactive optimists. Our Fuel letters taught us that a "get to" attitude is the earned default of those

RISE & SHINE

ave faced great adversity. But all of us can utilize "get to" as a powerful reminder to view our lives from a solid foundation of gratitude.

TEN GRATEFUL SONGS

- "Blessed" Brett Dennen
- "Portrait of an Artist as a Young Woman (Thank You)" Lizzie West & the White Buffalo
- "Be Here Now" Mason Jennings
- "Thank You (Falettinme Be Mice Elf Agin)" Sly & the Family Stone
- "Who I Am Today" Jason Mraz
- "Good Old Days" Ziggy Marley
- "Lie in Our Graves" Dave Matthews Band
- "What a Wonderful World" Louis Armstrong
- "Thank You" India.Arie
- "I Can't Wait" Ryan Montbleau

Read It and Reap

The field of psychology has traditionally been focused more on understanding distress and illness than on understanding wellness and positive emotions. Only in recent years has there been more systematic study of gratitude and its positive effects. The body of research is large and growing, and the findings support impressive conclusions about the strong links between gratitude, mental health, and well-being. The *Journal of Personality* and the journal *Personality and Individual Differences*—among other publications—have reported that grateful people are happier, more open and sociable, less depressed and neurotic, and express higher levels of satisfaction with their lives and relationships. Grateful people have higher levels of personal growth and self-acceptance, and they have stronger coping skills for the challenges and setbacks they experience. They also share a greater willingness to seek out help from others, spend more time planning how to address issues, and demonstrate the ability to interpret challenging events in ways that help them grow. In short, the data confirm there is nothing but upside to practicing gratitude—but see for yourself. Your body, mind, and spirit will thank you.

Thanksgiving

Personally, we are grateful for water, mountains, freedom, music, road trips, March Madness, laughter, and the chance to take a chance. Above all, we are grateful for our family and friends.

To quote Alex, we don't know how to describe it other than to say we love them. That shared love and appreciation for others in your life—for your "family," by any definition—may be the most nourishing source of gratitude there is.

I'm sure that's why Thanksgiving is our favorite holiday, by far. It's really a feast of the superpowers: simplicity (stripped of the gifts and excessive hype that can weigh down other holidays), love (of course), and humor among them. But gratitude reigns supreme on this holiday. Young and old, everyone gets it: We gather to give thanks.

The Dark and the Light

In the days that followed the terrorist attacks on the World Trade Center on September 11, 2001, much of the country was in shock. As a nation, we wrestled with a mix of anger, pain, and sorrow. Everyone was also tremendously grateful for the heroic efforts and sacrifices of the New York firefighters, police, and all other public servants, in response to that horrific act.

Personally, we lost friends in the attacks. It was a dark time. At work, many wondered aloud if it made sense to be shipping Life is Good products out at all. We held a company-wide meeting to connect, heal, and discuss that very subject. At one point, a quiet woman from our shipping team raised her hand, and asked, "What if we created a fundraising T-shirt to help the victims and their families?"

Later that week, we sent out a message to all our retail partners (numbering about a thousand at the time), informing them that 100 percent of the profits from a special, stylized American flag shirt would be donated to the cause. The emphatic response was an influx of orders that boosted morale, led to welcome round-the-clock shifts, and gave our entire team a sense of united purpose. Instead of feeling helpless, as we all did at the time, we were able to help, in our own small way. Surprisingly, we blew past our initial fundraising goal of $20,000 and were eventually able to donate $207,000 to help the victims and their families. It was a galvanizing project for our team to print and ship all those shirts, and it felt good. That feeling would help to shape our decisions and actions in the years to come.

> The stronger the wind, the stronger the trees.
> —Douglas Malloch

The whole experience confirmed for us that even—in fact, *especially*—in the darkest times, people are drawn to the light. We mourn what we've lost, but we cherish what we still have. We all want to help make things better. We saw it in our team, in our business partners, and in the country as a whole.

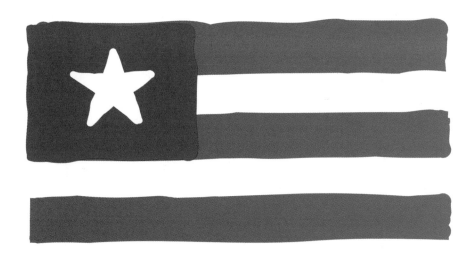

Life is good.

FUEL:
GRATITUDE

Dear Life is Good,

My name is Nancy Suhr, and I am the widow of firefighter Daniel Thomas Suhr of Engine 216, who was killed September 11, 2001, in the attacks on the World Trade Center in New York. I am writing to tell you how much I love all of your products and how for me it's like having a piece of Dan with me when I drink from your mugs or wear a T-shirt that says "Life is good."

You see, that was Dan's motto in life. We met in grade school. He was my first boyfriend. Let's just say he was my first everything! Tragedy struck Dan and his family more than once over the years. His brother Ed, a 21-year-old graduate of West Point, was left a paraplegic after a car accident. He was hospitalized for 17 months, and Dan drove from Brooklyn to the Bronx VA hospital every afternoon after work to feed Ed. (Ed is now married with twin boys.) Not long after, Dan's sister, a New York City police officer, had a car accident that left her in a coma with a major brain injury. With all Dan had lived through, when people would ask him how he was doing he'd say, "Life is good." You see, to Dan, the important thing was that his brother and sister were still part of his life.

Around the time we were engaged, Dan became a fire-
fighter. He was thrilled, just like his father who was a firefighter
before him. We got married and he had a job he loved. He'd tell
me that if we ever won the lottery, I could quit my job but he
would stay a firefighter. We opened a pizza store together and
wanted to start a family. It took us four long years and a cou-
ple of surgeries for me to conceive. But thank God it worked,
because I now have our beautiful daughter to keep me say-
ing "Life is good." Briana was two when he was killed. Since
Danny was taken from us, we've had to endure some rough
times even still, including emergency surgery for her when she
was six and my breast cancer diagnosis at age 41. God was
good, and I'm perfectly fine now! To say we've had an interest-
ing life doesn't quite cut it, but through it all we try our best to
remember that so many people have it worse than we do. On a
whole, our Life is good. We appreciate all the kindness that was
bestowed upon us since Dan's death. We miss him every min-
ute of every day. He was a great dad, my best friend, and my
husband. I am one of the lucky people who was really loved by

the person I was sharing my life with. Our daughter will never know the amazing man who wanted her so much and loved her with his whole heart. But she will know how much he loved life and lived like every second was his last.

Every year at Christmas we give everybody on both sides of the family—adults, children, and babies—a Life is Good T-shirt from Danny, so they can remember his motto—and maybe, when things get tough, remember to hang in there. Life has a way of turning around, and you must find the good in each day because life is fragile. Live like Danny did—full throttle. He loved life and packed a lot of living into his short 37 years.

I want to thank you from the bottom of my heart for helping me to continue to give a little piece of Danny to all the people he loved. And when it gets unbearable, I just put on my Life is Good T-shirt and remember when my life was really, really good and I can smile. So thank you for helping to ease our pain by your beautiful and inspiring products. May God bless all of you and your families always!

Sincerely,
Nancy and Briana Suhr
and forever Danny

THREE WAYS TO MAKE A GRATITUDE ADJUSTMENT

1. **PUMP YOUR OWN FUEL.** Is there any substitute for a hand-written note or card of appreciation? Email, texts—they work too. It's a matter of taking the time to express something beyond the generic, and truly personalizing your authentic gratitude. What comes from the heart goes to the heart. When you share your appreciation for someone's unique qualities or specific impact on your life, you make yourself and the ones you care about happier.

2. **"GET TO."** Use this powerful phrase to reframe the ordinary "have tos" you might otherwise view as burdens or bland checklist items. We all "get to" be here on this planet in the first place—so much of our experience depends on how we choose to view it. Try placing a jar on the kitchen counter at home, and anytime someone gets caught saying, "I have to . . ." they need to put a dollar in the jar for groceries. Do the same at the office for beer money or a donation to your favorite cause. Gratitude adjustments will follow.

3. **CELEBRATE THANKSGIVING 365.** A natural time for us to pause and give thanks is before we share a meal together, whether it's a sandwich or a home-cooked feast. Take a few deep breaths, hold hands if you like, and share some things you're grateful for. It helps diffuse stress, reconnect with each other, and prepare our bodies to enjoy whatever vittles lie before us.

Half Full

Optimists gather to make some joy at a Life is Good Festival in 2011.

The Good Doctor

In the 1950s, little kids in the United States had a problem on their hands—and so did their parents and teachers. Most of the books written for children at that time were incredibly boring. The standard Dick and Jane primers were stale snoozers that created no compelling reason for kids to dive back in and develop their reading skills. Enter the Good Doctor.

Ted Geisel (aka Dr. Seuss) wrote *The Cat in the Hat* in 1957 as a direct effort to expel the tedium of Dick and Jane from school libraries and family bookshelves. Spurred on by a challenge from the director of Houghton Mifflin's educational division, he set out to "write a story first graders can't put down."

Seuss met that challenge and many more to come, forever changing the game of children's lit. His secret was to infuse his books with an irresistible fun factor, which augmented his sage and prophetic messaging. The positive impact of his prolific publishing output, spanning a remarkable seven decades, is unparalleled. Thank you, Doc!

Seuss inspired so many of us from an early age to unlock our imaginations (*If I Ran the Circus*), open our minds (*Green Eggs and Ham*), and embrace adventure (*Oh, the Places You'll Go!*). He also used his own potent imagination to deliver powerful social commentary for all ages. Timeless works like *How the Grinch Stole Christmas!* (on materialism) and *The Lorax* (on sustainability) manage to communicate profound, universal advice to humanity—advice even young children can begin to grasp—without ever getting preachy or talking down to readers.

How the Oobleck did the Good Doctor pull *that* off? The man had a paintbrush and a killer wisdom beard, but what Seuss had most of all was FUN. He brought it into every page and spread it to the world, one wocket, wumbus, and bippo-no-bungus at a time.

Deep messages are woven into works like *The Sneetches and Other Stories,* a book Seuss published in 1961 that eloquently deals with discrimination and cultural obsessions with physical appearance. But why our repeat reaches for the lessons it teaches—even a

Dr. Seuss at his operating table in La Jolla, California, in 1979

half century later? The *fun* way it's told makes the story irresistible. The combination of peculiar illustrations, inventive wordplay, and a rhythmic roller coaster of rhymes is masterfully magnetic.

No fun in the writer, no fun in the reader. Seuss made kids' books fun and enjoyable *for parents and teachers* as well as for kids, and as a result, that joy still gets transmitted to the tiniest tots at bed-times around the globe.

Good for You

Fun is irresistible at every age. More than just frivolous, it is often the spark that connects and inspires us to feel most united and alive. Fun is also just plain good for you. Good for your health, as a stress reliever, immunity booster, and body rejuvenator. *"Oh, the Thinks you can Think"* when that stress is low and you're enjoying yourself. Fun takes many forms but it's unmistakable: When you feel it, you know. We've said optimism is a courageous choice—and sometimes recharging that optimism demands that we get out and seek out our own simple fun.

As little kids, most of us are drawn to the silly and spontaneous. If we're lucky, physical fun is on the daily menu—from running, jumping, and splashing to drawing, building, and pretend play. As grown-ups, that menu tends to shrink, and we can find ourselves "picking our spots" to have fun only at certain times, such as weekends, or at certain events, such as parties. The trick is to actually prioritize fun, and weave it into who we are. It's not a dessert reserved for our special occasions; it's a healthy part of the main course.

FIVE FUN CONTEMPORARY KIDS' BOOKS

- *The Day the Crayons Quit* by Drew Daywalt and Oliver Jeffers
- *If I Built a House* by Chris Van Dusen
- *Journey* by Aaron Becker
- *The Whale and the Snail* by Julia Donaldson
- *An Awesome Book!* by Dallas Clayton

Let It Fly

People like Dr. Seuss and our mom (a strong tag team) showed us early on that fun doesn't require much beyond a playful, open mind. A ball doesn't hurt either. Our whole lives, we've been drawn to any kind of sphere we can throw and catch. A ball is the ultimate connector. What starts out in childhood as a game of catch (rubber ball, ball of tape, baseball) can remain a kinetic link to other humans (friends or strangers) for a lifetime. A ball means fun, with no language required. Frisbees, we've found, have the very same effect. Any time we're playing on a field or beach, we love surprising a stranger with a little eye contact and quick flick of the disc. The smile percentage is high, and the connection is downright childlike. And doglike. Throw. Catch. Connect.

We are lucky to be part of a community of friends and family that recognizes and celebrates the electric power of physical play. One of our favorite traditions of the year is an annual Ultimate Frisbee tournament we play around Thanksgiving time called Marie's Cup, named after a very special aunt who tragically left us too soon. It's been 18 years of hard-fought battles between extended family members and a band of nonfamily hooligans known as the "Outsiders." The long tourneys of contact, loose-rules Frisbee football in erratic New England weather have delivered some vintage moments over the years. The real magic, however, always unfolds well after the final touchdown. Both teams drop into our parents' basement for cold beer, hot food, and a preposterous parade of poorly sung parody songs. Backed by the "house band" (some with legit skills), players get up to celebrate, skewer, or serenade the jam-packed crowd in the unfinished basement, surrounded by Dad's endless books, board games, and power tools.

As on-field skills have declined, our overall song quality has followed suit. "The worser the better," we all agree, and the home crowd is very forgiving. It's deep social connection through fun in the form of Frisbee, comedy, and music. It's also fun, a few decades after college, to invite folks to a kegger in your parents' basement.

Over the years we've developed other savored traditions that we refuse to let go of, no matter how busy life gets. The Homeslice Film Festival happens every two years, with friends who have no idea how to make movies delivering their best efforts in the form of a mercifully brief (eight minutes max) film. A few true gems always arise, but every single film adds to the for-the-hell-of-it spirit of the night.

As adults, we can all benefit from (not so much finding time, but) *making* time for fun in our lives. That means recognizing fun's unique power to help us retain a youthful enthusiasm, and committing to it even when our calendars appear packed with more serious business.

Life is Good Festivals

If fun has the power to draw people together, as we've witnessed throughout our lives, why not draw them together for a good cause?

In 2003, we took our first large-scale crack at doing just that. Children have always been Life is Good's ultimate inspiration. Guided by their spontaneous spirit and the motivation of our Fuel community, we did what any sound-minded leaders of a fledgling T-shirt business would do. We hosted a pumpkin festival.

In fact, for the next four years, we hosted Life is Good Pumpkin Festivals in several locations, using one simple, silly, and unifying goal to rally communities around a very serious cause: attempting to break the Guinness World Record for most carved, lit jack-o'-lanterns in one place at one time.

We had little clue how to scale such events, but once again we learned that "the work will teach you how to do it." We teamed with a great Maine-based nonprofit called Camp Sunshine, which supports children facing life-threatening illnesses and their families. The first year we were stunned by the turnout of more than 10,000 people rolling out of their trucks filled with pumpkins and ready to carve their contributions.

We offered simple throwback games like sack races, home run derby, and obstacle courses for kids and grown-ups alike. Each year the crowds, the official count of lit pumpkins, and the fundraising numbers grew. Eventually, in 2006 on the Boston Common, the nation's oldest public park, a huge festival crowd managed to carve and light 30,128 pumpkins to break the world record together. More importantly, we raised great awareness and over $500,000 that day for Camp Sunshine.

One of the best parts of those early fests was watching people search the winding pumpkin rows and pumpkin towers (the largest one 40 feet high) for their own personalized carvings to show their friends. People could look up at nightfall and say, "Wow, I was a part of something beautiful that happened today."

The first festivals confirmed what we had hoped: Fun is like a jack-o'-lantern itself. We have to work sometimes to keep it flickering. Especially in the harder times, we are all drawn to that light and to one another. We all want to be part of something positive—sometimes it just takes a little fun to bring us together.

In 2007, we rented Fenway Park, home of the Boston Red Sox, in a new fest quest to crown the "World's Greatest Backyard

October in Maine is not typically bikini weather, but anything goes at a Life is Good Pumpkin Festival. (Yes, she's about 13 months pregnant.) Life is Good Pumpkin Festival, 2003

Life is Good's Pumpkin Logistics Coordinator considers next steps.

Better to light 30,128 pumpkins than curse the darkness: The LIG community breaks a world record to help kids in need in 2006.

Athlete." Fundraisers competed in seed spitting, throwing Frisbees off the "Green Monster" (Fenway's 37-foot-tall left field wall), and playing Wiffle Ball home run derby in center field (fulfilling many diehard Sox fans' dreams).

The festival crowd has a ball and raises $802,636 for kids in need: Life is Good at Fenway Park in July 2007.

As the festivals evolved, each one confirmed how powerful the fun factor could be in drawing people to a good cause. There are many inspiring examples of this exploding trend, from the growth of the Movember campaign (working to "change the face of men's health" one moustache at a time) to the wild viral success of the Ice Bucket Challenge for ALS research that took off in 2014. Just as Dr. Seuss had turned the serious work of literacy learning into fun, we're all learning new ways to turn fundraising into fun raising.

Over the years, music became a central unifying ingredient in our festivals as world-class musicians like Jack Johnson, Dave Matthews, and The Roots stepped up to help the cause. The unique combo of inspiring music mixed with interactive art, physical games for all ages, an optimistic vibe, and all-for-one purpose that helps set the Life is Good Fests apart. Tattoos mix seamlessly with strollers at these one-of-a-kind events. One hundred percent of all profits raised by LIG Festivals (totaling over $11 million, to date) have been donated to help kids overcome violence, poverty, and severe medical challenges. Raising awareness and funds for a serious cause doesn't have to be serious. Fun is the magnet that draws us all to the meaning. We think the Good Doctor would agree.

TEN FUN SONGS

- "Say Hey (I Love You)" Michael Franti & Spearhead
- "Uptown Funk!" Mark Ronson featuring Bruno Mars
- "City" Thao & The Get Down Stay Down
- "The Minx" The New Mastersounds
- "The Oogum Boogum Song" Brenton Wood
- "Hey Ya!" Outkast
- "Good Day" Nappy Roots
- "Put Your Records On" Corinne Bailey Rae
- "What'd I Say" Ray Charles
- "Hurricane Season" Trombone Shorty

Pages 152–157: The little things are the big things: In addition to world-class music, Life is Good Festivals feature an array of fun, including dog agility and BMX bike shows, interactive art exhibits, and old-fashioned games for all ages.

FUEL:
FUN

Left anonymously on the festival grass, this is one of our shortest and favorite Fuel "letters" ever received. Addressed to no one, it is therefore addressed to everyone who decided to focus on (and grow) the good for a day.

Blur the Line

Having fun at work is not a diversion from productivity. In fact, it's an essential ingredient to staying loose, open, creative, and solution-oriented. Fun makes for easy lifting. You can have strong ideas, great products, and a brilliant team—but fun (once again) is the grease on the chain that keeps the whole bike rolling. Often viewed as frivolous frosting in the world of business, fun is actually a wildly effective means to attract, unite, and propel people toward achieving common goals. What worked at early street fairs, and later at the fests, is an integral part of our work culture at Life is Good today.

As a result, we make sure that large signature events help everyone feel informed and connected to our mission and each other. Our biggest are the semiannual, company-wide Jake Jams, which always include a strong mix of comedy, live music from our all-employee house band, and open-book updates from leadership. Skits have taken the form of game shows, mock fashion runway shows, karaoke sing-alongs, and more. One memorable jam pitted our VP of finance against our in-house attorney—neither position generally known for hilarity—in a boxing-themed "comedy smackdown" involving outlandish promoters, ringside trainers, cross-dressing ring girls, and a frenzied voting "panel" made up of everyone in the room. Other gatherings include summer picnics with outdoor games and live music, and winter snow-tubing expeditions at a local mountain outside Boston. We try to spread that same childlike fun on the road as well, whether it's chucking discs into the crowd at speaking engagements, tossing footballs in the aisles at trade shows, or weaving physical games into our visits with business partners.

More important than these special occasions is the everyday fun we can all bring to each other at work. It starts with your own

Blur the line between
WORK AND PLAY

energy: realizing that a simple quick story, ball throw, or one-liner can defuse stress, reconnect teammates, and refresh our collective "get to" mindset. Maintaining a childlike appetite for fun every day is healthy, enjoyable, and good for business.

Believe it or not, Life is Good days are not all filled with Frisbees and ice cream. Like any business, we work hard to manage our P&Ls while fulfilling our mission, and that can be intense. Through the highs and lows, we strive to be true to our brand name, lifting each other with bursts of fun when they're needed most. It's a shared, conscious, and healthy way to blur the line between work and play.

> Give the world a reason to dance.
> —*Kid President*

Try This at Home

Dr. Seuss inspired us to believe that growing up doesn't ever have to mean giving up on silliness and fun. Studies show that connecting to your childlike energy and joy can be particularly challenging in midlife, as people balance the responsibilities of parenthood, their own aging parents, and increased work demands. Fun often takes a backseat, so it requires a conscious decision to keep it right alongside you, riding shotgun with the windows down.

Regardless of what stage you're at on your own precious ride, consider the following suggestions to shift fun into high gear for the road ahead.

THREE WAYS TO BRING ON THE FUN

1. **CUSTOMIZE.** Fun is subjective. To reconnect to what brings you the most joy, you can go all the way back to childhood (Making things? Laughing with friends? Pretending or playing games outside? Inside?). That stuff is pretty hardwired, and chances are some variation on the theme can jump-start that childlike energy in you. You can also look back at the past week or month and ask, "What (and who) spiked my fun factor?" A new hobby (especially shared) like cooking, dancing, or home-brewing is a good formula, but the answer can often be making time for the fun you already love. Carve out that night to play games or just hang with friends. Shut your phone down for a few hours. Dust off the guitar case, craft kit, or card table. Simply spending time with friends who bring their own fun energy is priceless.

2. **GET A MOVE ON.** We all know physical exercise is good for us, for endless reasons. Why not find some form that's actually fun for you? All kinds of group workouts are emerging on the scene, like fitness boot camps and new variations on CrossFit, BoxFit, yoga, and Pilates. If this sounds more like work to you, how 'bout a soccer, kickball, or dodgeball league? Bocce won't sculpt your frame, but it's a great game. The positive trend toward these group activities underscores our need to connect with others and just have a good time. If organized team sports and games are not your thing, just have a ball. With you. Always. Bounce it, say hello with it, kick off meetings with it. Throw. Catch. Connect.

3. **LET LOOSE.** Sir Ernest Shackleton's famous Antarctic expedition involved fun as more than an icebreaker. He kept his 27 men alive for almost two years through unimaginable hardships, in part by keeping them loose under extremely challenging conditions. For Sir Ernest's

crew, fun was sing-alongs, hockey games, and occasional ballroom dancing for comic relief. Everybody has stress in their life, and bursts of fun throughout the day help keep your mind and spirit strong. The random belted lyric across the office floor. The absurd kitchen dance for his or her eyes only. The silly rhymes, tag game, or inventive fist bumps with a child. Crank up the music, try out a strange new voice and a song verse—good or bad (remember, the worser the better). Weave more of those little moments into your day, because the world and the people around you need them more than you realize.

COMPA

ASSION

one tribe

We Are One

Compassion is the concern for and willingness to help someone who is suffering. Identifying with another person—including identifying with their pain—is hardwired in us. In recent years, neuroscientists have confirmed that our brain exhibits a similar pain response to another's suffering as it does to our own. Conversely, when we give to or help others, a circuit in the brain is activated and makes us feel good. So in the simplest terms, science indicates that there is a powerful connection between helping other people and feeling happy. How cool is that?

Clearly, when T-shirt guys start talking about neuroscience, it's time to reel it in. The point is: We humans feel the pain of others deeply. We're herd animals. So we're driven to reach out where we can and try to alleviate the suffering of others.

> You'll come to see suffering that will break your heart. When it happens, and it will, don't turn away from it; turn toward it. That is the moment when change is born.
> —*Melinda Gates*

Carry On

The links between compassion and our own humanity go back tens of thousands of years. In the 1950s, the skeletal remains of a severely deformed Neanderthal man presumed to be in his late 40s were discovered in the mountains of Iraq. Scientists wondered how a person—deformed since birth—could have survived for more than 40 years in a grueling hunter-gatherer society without being able to walk. The answer: His tribe carried him. Can you imagine trying to hunt, gather, and avoid saber-toothed tigers, all while literally carrying a grown Neanderthal man? Without performance sneakers or moisture-wicking fabrics? What could possibly motivate such seemingly impractical, burdensome behavior? You guessed it. Compassion.

Give What You Can

In our hyperconnected world, exposure to all forms of global suffering can be overwhelming. How can we possibly address all the tragedies and injustices that are part of the 24/7 news cycle? The answer is: We can't. What we can do is care for those in our circle. We can seek to understand and help those we know and love who might be suffering. We can do the same for strangers in our neighborhoods or at our work. Beyond that, we can choose broader causes that align with our personal values and passions. How much you choose to do is not what matters most. Everyone's resources are different, so only you will know how much giving and helping is the right amount for you.

Make It Easy

During Life is Good's first six years in business, our revenue had grown from $78 to more than $3 million, and we started working with several charities regularly. They were all great causes, but the decisions about who to support were based more on who came knocking than anything else. If somebody asked and we had some money or time, we gave it to them, but our methods were random and inefficient. We realized that in order to maximize our positive impact, we needed to zoom in on a single social cause that aligned closely with the philosophies of our company.

Kids are the ultimate optimists. Life is Good has always been about bringing out the kid in all of us, regardless of age, so helping them was a natural path for us. As we continued to pursue that idea, our employees got involved. As time passed, they became even more excited about helping kids than making T-shirts. Can you blame them? The natural connection made our new cause easy for customers to understand; when we held festivals or designed special T-shirts to help kids, they loved it and supported us. That made things easier for us too.

Joy Clinics

As it happened, in 1989—the same year we started making T-shirts—an inspiring friend of ours had begun building a trail-blazing nonprofit called Project Joy, focused on the social and emotional health of Boston's most vulnerable children. Steve Gross, the founder, is one of the most compassionate people we know. He's devoted his entire adult life to the healthy development of children facing the most challenging circumstances. A pioneer in using play to promote resiliency in children and their caregivers, he's also a revered leader in the field of early childhood trauma response.

In the early 1990s, when we were in Boston in between road trips, we had helped Steve by designing logos and T-shirts, painting gyms, and helping to run fundraiser hoop tourneys. By 2000, as we were developing our own approach to social work through trial and error, we noticed some clear parallels between our focus and the great work Steve was doing. Although his organization was dealing with some dark forces affecting children, they were bringing joy: smiles, laughter, bouncing balls, running, climbing, clapping, dancing, singing. Although Steve and his team were well educated about the problems, they weren't fixated on the problems. They were focused on solutions. Project Joy was a group of powerful proactive optimists, and they were going into neighborhoods and hospitals where optimism is needed most.

> The grass is greener where you water it.
> —*Unknown*

One day, as we were discussing all this, Steve said, "Isn't it crazy that there are thousands of trauma clinics across our country, but zero joy clinics?" This is where we really started seeing the potential for a match with Life is Good.

Helping the Helpers

By 2005, Project Joy had evolved from providing direct care for children to a unique and innovative approach that trained and cared for the caregivers: those men and women who were dedicating their lives to helping children grow up safe, loved, and joyful. The organization had learned their impact would grow by helping the helpers, and that focus was born out of Steve's deep compassion for the exceedingly difficult work of frontline caregivers. Many, like inner-city early childhood educators, counselors, foster care providers, or child life specialists, are not highly compensated for the important work they do. Their daily work is physically and emotionally

When

it

rains

it

shines

draining, and their spirits can be assaulted by the heartbreaking realities in front of them: young children who are grappling with the devastating traumas of poverty, violence, abuse, neglect, and severe medical challenges.

Project Joy training was providing early childhood professionals with concrete tools and techniques to implement in their daily work. They also provided a rare opportunity for caregivers to

Steve Gross, Chief Playmaker at Life is Good, inspires wherever he goes with his unique blend of wit, wisdom, and compassion.

experience connection, play, and joy in ways that replenished their spirits and strengthened their resolve. A central emphasis became learning self-care, so that these unsung frontline heroes could sustain themselves over the long haul. After all, the best way for child care providers to help children discover confidence and inspiration in life is to nourish these qualities in themselves. As a wise man once said: "Beware the naked man who offers you his shirt." You can't give what you don't have.

Although kids had always inspired us as the ultimate arms-wide-open optimists, Steve and Project Joy helped us to see that many children struggle with terrible forces that threaten to crush that optimism early in their lives. As we made our mistakes and took our lumps in business, our old friend was making his way too. Each time we visited with him, we were more impressed with the common ground between the missions of Life is Good and Project Joy. As our business continued to expand, we made larger commitments each year to support Project Joy—and each year, more of our good people at Life is Good expressed their support. We started to imagine how we might bring our organizations together as one.

Playmakers

In early 2010, both companies had dated long enough and were ready to get married. We absorbed Project Joy into the Life is Good Kids Foundation and renamed it The Playmakers. Why "Playmakers"? In sports, a playmaker is someone who steps up and makes a winning contribution at a critical time in the game. Similarly, a Playmaker is a person who makes a positive, life-changing impact at a critical time in a child's life. A Playmaker is a difference maker, a compassionate game changer in the life of a child.

From that day forward, Playmakers has been central to our non-profit initiatives. Their offices are right in the center of our company's headquarters in Boston, so that we're able to work and play together every day. Most important, we weave our social purpose into everything we do.

Ten Percent for Kids

As a clear sign of our commitment to that social purpose, we announced publicly that 10 percent of our annual profits are given to helping kids in need. The message gets through to all our customers, but it's also a healthy, galvanizing point of difference for

A young girl in Gulfport, Mississippi, reclaims her confidence and smile after Hurricane Katrina, thanks in part to her teacher, a certified Playmaker.

our staff. Employees know that, no matter what part of the business they touch, their work contributes to healing and strengthening vulnerable children.

Today, there are more than 5,000 Life is Good Playmaker-trained and –supported professionals throughout the United States and Haiti, caring for more than 100,000 children a day.

Business Is Good

Not Only for Profits, Triple Bottom Liners, Conscious Capitalists, B Corporations: Many labels are used today to describe businesses that are trying to help people, animals, and the planet. Businesses in this category involve a greater depth and commitment than

From left: Bert, John, Shawn White, Kerrie Gross, Rich Cremin, and Roy Heffernan became business partners in 2005 with a shared commitment to help kids in need.

those offering "cause-related marketing," "corporate social responsibility," or "giving back." In the first group, social causes are strategically integrated across all facets of the businesses. In practice, this means that purposes beyond making profit—feeding a hungry child or protecting our waterways—become essential to the organization's success.

The good news is that this category of business is on the rise. As long as consumers continue to vote with their dollars about the social causes that matter most to them, the businesses that positively impact the world are only going to grow in numbers and in strength.

Self-Compassion

The Life is Good Playmakers' philosophy of "You can't share what you don't have" provides vital direction for those whose lives require an abundance of compassion. In order to consistently help others, you need to take care of yourself. You may be in a "helping profession" like teaching, nursing, counseling, and the like. You may find yourself at a stage of life that requires an abundance of compassionate response and care. Maybe you're the parent of young children, caring for aging parents or an ill family member, or responding to someone suffering from depression or a hurtful loss. Whatever the scenario, tending to our own joy and well-being is crucial. Breathing techniques, meditation, yoga, play, recreational exercise, and scheduling downtime are all simple, smart, and beneficial ways to achieve this.

Social support is also essential. Spend time with those who bring you positive personal energy, and who help you see the glass as half full. They can help you keep a balanced worldview and remind you that your own compassionate actions do make a difference.

> If you want others to be happy, practice compassion. If you want to be happy, practice compassion.
> —*Dalai Lama XIV*

Just Like Me

We do like simple phrases. Much like "Yes, and" helps us open our minds and "Get to" helps us practice gratitude, the words "Just like me" can be a strong tool in cultivating our compassion for others. It's a traditional Buddhist practice of framing our interactions. Friend, foe, or stranger—each person we meet is dealing with some level of struggle in his or her life. The practice reminds us "Just like me, this person wants to be happy . . . Just like me, this person has known sadness, suffering, and despair."

TEN SONGS OF COMPASSION

- "You Are Not Alone" Mavis Staples
- "The Weight" The Band
- "A Little Bit of Everything" Dawes
- "High Tide or Low Tide" Bob Marley
- "If There Was No You" Brandi Carlisle
- "Join Together" The Who
- "Us" Brother Ali
- "Let It Go" Michael Franti & Spearhead
- "Shelter From the Storm" Bob Dylan
- "Lean on Me" Bill Withers

This perspective comes pretty easily when we engage with loved ones, and less so when such relationships are strained. It can also affect ordinary exchanges with strangers. How about the checkout woman overwhelmed by the long, impatient line of customers? Are you the one sighing your frustration from the back of the line, or the one who can lift her with empathy and a kind word when you reach the checkout? Just like you, other people can use every dose of compassion they can get. By lifting others, we can lower the shields many of us raise against the outside world as we grow older.

When it comes to our most contentious relationships, "Just like me" can help us break down barriers, avoid sliding into combative positions, and find common ground and resolution.

FUEL:
COMPASSION

Dear Playmakers,

After returning from the Playmaker training for child life specialists, I felt refreshed and rejuvenated as well as inspired and excited to use all that I learned. I was tested almost immediately with a very difficult case at my hospital.

I had begun working very closely with a set of six-year-old fraternal twins, "Michael" and "Jess." The twins were in a horrific car fire and hospitalized for extensive second- and third-degree burns on their chest, face, legs, and hands. Even more upsetting was the fact that this car fire was set intentionally by their own mother in a dual suicide/homicide attempt. Needless to say, the playful, joyful approach advocated by Playmakers as a way to create deep connections and facilitate healing did not come to the front of my mind as I set out to do child life interventions with them.

However, I was quickly surprised by Michael, the precocious and inquisitive, yet protective older twin. Michael was brought into the hydrotherapy room, or "tank room," daily for burn cleaning and dressing changes. He was frequently distressed by the thought of this procedure, as it is long and quite painful. I knew this would be the perfect opportunity to work closely with him to relieve his pain and anxiety. I brainstormed some ideas not only to divert him from the pain, but also to find a way to connect with Michael and have him connect with the technicians helping him.

Almost immediately I thought of "Magic Ball." Since Michael could not move from the tank table to express his own moves, he used the Magic Ball to be in total control of mine. "Magic Ball, Magic Ball, do the robot!" he would say and I would do my best robot moves. "Magic Ball, Magic Ball, do the twist!" "Magic Ball, Magic Ball, do the silly dance!" His happiness and delight grew, as did his distraction.

Then came an imaginative idea that took the cake. "Magic Ball, Magic Ball, CONGA LINE!" The room instantly turned into a party-like atmosphere. All the staff members, burn technicians, the child life specialist, the child life intern, and the nurses jumped on the conga line and snaked throughout the tank room and beyond. Michael was sitting up on the bed, his burns exposed, but smiling and laughing

SOMETIMES THE
BEST CONVERSATION IS
A GAME OF CATCH.

nonstop! He was able not only to gain some control in this situation, but also to be entertained by the very staff people who before he perceived as the people "who hurt me." The benefits of this intervention are innumerable and great. Michael actually looked forward to getting his dressings changed from this point on.

In the course of Michael's treatment I implemented many more Playmaker games, activities, and techniques that provided both comfort and connection. This experience, along with all the Playmaker techniques I am using, have essentially transformed my career forever. Not only have I learned about myself and how to remain joyful and engaged even in the saddest of situations, but I learned from Michael how to keep positive in the face of adversity. I have strengthened my practice and deepened my passion for helping children in need.

The Life is Good Playmakers has been a blessing, and I don't think I can express exactly how grateful I am for the amazing group of people who have facilitated my growth as a Playmaker and professional!

Danielle
Playmaker and
Child Life Specialist

THREE WAYS TO PRACTICE COMPASSION

1. **HELP YOURSELF.** Remember, compassion begins with kindness to yourself. Make peace of mind a priority. Take time for yourself. Learn to disarm your internal critic by accepting who you are today. Be patient with your stumblings, and don't dwell on past mistakes. Forgive yourself and move on, with a positive eye toward the future. If you're struggling through difficult stuff, you may want to enlist the help of a personal coach or a counselor, or give one of the healing arts—like yoga, meditation, and mindfulness practices—a try. Develop self-awareness as a foundation from which you can genuinely understand and empathize with others.

2. **JUST LIKE ME.** Cultivate your compassion with that simple phrase "Just like me . . ." Just like you, everyone else is fighting some battle, big or small. Just like you, others want to be happy and free of suffering. Keep this in mind as you meet friends and strangers alike—and especially if you're working on a strained relationship. Remember that even those who seem to "have it all together," and those who simply drive you nuts, face challenges you don't fully understand. This broad view enables you to rise above petty squabbles, break down barriers, and more easily seize opportunities to help others.

3. **GIVE PRESENCE.** Don't feel as though you need to have all the answers to be of help to someone who's hurting. Just be yourself and take the time to be with them. Your presence can be more powerful than you think. The action of physically being with someone when they're hurting can make all the difference in the world.

Common ground

CREAT

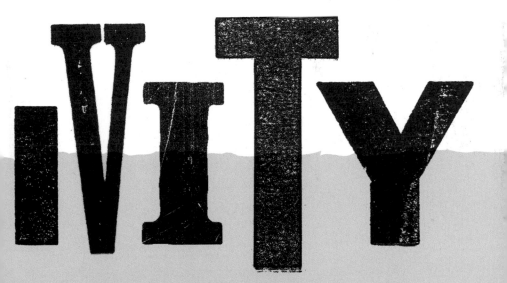

Getting Better

The Beatles started out as a cover band (don't we all?) and went on to become, well, The Beatles. What can we mere mortals possibly learn from the legends of Liverpool? The versatility of men's haircuts? The joys of strawberries and submarines? The timeless ideals of peace, love, and togetherness? Of course. We can also learn a great deal about creativity: how to access it and how to set it free.

As the Fab Four evolved from mop-top "Love Me Do" heartthrobs touring the globe in the mid-1960s to groundbreaking masters of their craft, they birthed an unprecedented album: *Sgt. Pepper's Lonely Hearts Club Band.* Beatlemania had been a wild ride for the four young mates of modest means. In 1966, the boys decided to stop touring. Their hiatus from the spotlight led the media to start sniping at them, declaring the band all but finished. Meanwhile, behind the scenes, The Beatles knew they were far from dried up. They were, in fact, elevating their collective game to new levels in Abbey Road Studio Two, meticulously molding a creative masterpiece. *Sgt. Pepper's,* released in 1967, was received immediately as a massive critical and commercial success. It has since been credited with elevating rock-and-roll to the level of fine art; in 2003, *Rolling Stone* magazine ranked it at #1 on its list of the "500 Greatest Albums of All Time."

Well played, lads. Well played.

Well Played

Our cousins' basement in Worcester, Massachusetts, was a special childhood cave where we did our best to create competitive games out of balls, drumsticks, elastics, and an ever morphing list of ambiguous rules. It's also, thanks to our cousins Rick and Pete, the first place we ever heard *Sgt. Pepper's*. Their family was ahead of us musically and intellectually—they always will be—but our crews share a deep bond formed over annual Thanksgiving meals and decades of bad fashion growing up. Their main basement room was magical simply because it was a blank canvas—an empty 15-by-15-foot arena where adults made very rare appearances. We were free to fumble over mysterious topics (like girls and *The Twilight Zone*), play games, and explore new ideas together.

At our ages—around 10 and 13 at the time—listening to each song on *Sgt. Pepper's* was like visiting a new planet. When we finally got our own copy back home, we played it over and over until every note (right down to "A Day in the Life's" final, striking single piano chord) was memorized. The Beatles, through their art, were taking us on wild new adventures of the mind.

Fresh Ground Pepper

We've never lost our admiration for what the Fab Four delivered. In our later years, curious to find out just how they created such musical brilliance, we discovered some crucial ingredients were at play.

One, their environment: The Beatles got out of their touring tunnel and exposed themselves to new surroundings and experiences to feed their creative minds. Two, they went for it: They utilized their fresh perspective and newfound freedom to take bold chances and invent their own methods of making art. Three, they shared and built upon each other's ideas to create something far greater than the sum of its parts.

The boys had a good long break—several months—to pursue personal interests before recording *Sgt. Pepper's*. That precious time

Life is good.

outside the intense Beatles bubble paid off when they reunited. George's exploration of classical Indian music and culture is one of the most famous examples. But each Beatle brought back his own unique seasonings to the "Pepper" stew. Paul mixed in vaudeville and show tunes; John brought some avant-garde poetry; Ringo and George focused on perfecting a wide range of instrumentation.

The whole album was built around the idea that recording it as a performance of their fictional alter egos—Sgt. Pepper's Lonely Hearts Club Band—would free The Beatles up to shed some skin and experiment with completely new compositions and musical styles. Knowing they wouldn't have to perform the songs live also helped create an environment ripe for brave new exploration at every stage of their co-creation.

> Creativity is intelligence having fun.
> —*Albert Einstein*

Announce the fictional Billy Shears to kick off the album? Sure. Inject some circus music for atmosphere? Absolutely. Add a chaotic stampede of animal sounds? Done. Forty-piece orchestra crescendos? Check. Use pocket combs wrapped in toilet paper as kazoos? Why not? Something about sharing their fresh perspectives with one another—and the fun and freedom of playing as a "new band" again—unlocked their imaginations and had the band (along with producer George Martin) in the ultimate innovative flow. Their foundational values remained firmly in place, but with the tighter reins of previous structures removed, their creative means of expressing those values exploded into new dimensions.

Collaboration was a big part of *Sgt. Pepper's* groundbreaking genius. Not only were songs fused together into one cohesive package like never before (with no standard gaps in between), but the band members fused their divergent individual interests into one strange, colorful concept album that has inspired millions.

Let It Flow

So how can the example of *Sgt. Pepper's* luminosity help light the way for our own creativity?

We can solve everyday puzzles and pursue our larger dreams in the same way great musicians blow our minds with their art: by feeding our childlike curiosity, daring to explore new ideas, and sharing those ideas collaboratively. This requires an adventurous spirit that can be hard for grown-ups to retain. We adults tend to fear the judgment of our peers far more than kids do. We're more sensitive to opinions. Whereas healthy children can scribble out a drawing and flash it proudly, adults tend to self-censor ideas, tapping the delete key all too early and often. Good musicians tend to be less inhibited by self-editing. They let their minds, voices, and fingers go, and let the music flow.

As kids, drawing cards and writing silly poems for friends and family, we got an early taste of how art can communicate ideas and connect people emotionally. We'd swap sketches and notes with

FIVE INSPIRING CREATIVES

- Christopher Guest (king of improv-fueled mockumentaries)
- Tina Fey (award-winning comedienne)
- Dave Eggers (keeps evolving Staggering skills while helping kids learn to write)
- The Avett Brothers (depth, unity, and damn good tunes)
- Wes Anderson (writer and director of comedic visual feasts)

Where There is art There is Love

each other and our other siblings all the time to impress, to challenge, or to make each other laugh. These days, we share sketches and notes with a larger team of incredibly talented and diverse artists from both inside and outside Life is Good. They are continually elevating and evolving the new ways we spread good vibes with every new season. Creativity wants out. Let it flow.

Picture yourself in a boat on a river,
with tangerine trees and marmalade skies.
—from "Lucy in the Sky With Diamonds"

Too trippy? OK, picture yourself in our office in Boston, with artwork all over and color wheel pies.

Still too trippy? All right, just come with us.

Creative Space

Just as kids who feel safe and loved are most open to play freely, adults in a "safe" creative environment (low on judgment, high on trust) are most open to play freely too. At Life is Good's creative hub in Beantown, we all do our best to foster a collective atmosphere of freedom, exploration, and collaboration.

Our creative team works in a wide-open studio on top of an old renovated factory building. Artists can be found sketching on couches, huddling around a kitchen table, or tucked in a nook painting watercolors. Our walls are covered with inspirational collages, from street art to album covers to seed bags. The urban digs strike a good balance of modern technology and old school charm. Artists or not, humans need open space and mind space. Our new-old brick home has a healthy dose of both.

You likely have places and activities that spark your best creative thinking: in the shower or garden; at your workbench or a cozy nook in your home or office; deep in the woods or whenever you're in motion—walking, running, or on your commute. Cherish that spark, relish its source, and go to it often.

Go Deep

To reinforce our values at LIG every day, we created a digital art gallery within our design center. It celebrates each superpower through inspirational images selected from our latest influences and most recent work. The images are always changing, but our core values are not. We've found that whether it's the family photos or a favorite painting you choose to hang in your hallway or the quotes you tape up on your walls, any reinforcement of what you live for, work for, or love fiercely lifts your spirit and energizes your physical space.

Every new season, we choose one superpower to highlight as our creative inspiration. As we formulate fresh ways to celebrate it, wanderings of feet and mind are strongly encouraged. We roam, we read, we live, and we view the subject through the lenses of our personal passions. Then we open up and riff on it with one another. We have to feel each superpower internally, and connect with it emotionally, before we can express it to our customers. (Once again, you can't give what you don't have.) When our team stays grounded in our values and adventurous in our approach, we know that our art has a great chance to connect, unite, and inspire people. That's what fires us up every day.

Your own positive impact multiplies when you're able to sync your creative pursuits with your existing values and passions. Think your housemates or neighbors have grown too distant? Or your apartment or neighborhood looks run down? Start the creative conversation about how the vibe or space gets revived, through a BBQ, cleanup, or game day. Believe kids' worlds are going a little too digital? Give 'em a fun alternative: Co-create a new obstacle course, word game, or kick-ass cardboard rocket ship.

Ideas Without Borders

Next time you're seeking creative solutions, try using a whiteboard or sticky notes to jot down a bunch of ideas, edit free. Get them all out, with the idea that for the moment, no idea is a bad one. We usually subscribe to a "Less is more" mantra, but in this forum (idea generation), the more, the better. The crazier, the better too. Let 'em all fly! *Then*, of course, you can shift into evaluation mode, cutting some ideas outright and building on some of your favorites. Having shared ideas openly, you now hold the creative clay from which to mold and refine your best answer.

Good to Not Know

Frustrated with a key relationship in your life? Stuck on a problem at work or home that seems insurmountable? The first key to creative

solutions is admitting you don't know the answer. That frees us to ask openly, engage, and listen so we can co-create the answer instead of butting heads or defending our own fraction of a solution.

It's right to be wrong. Start being wrong and suddenly anything is possible. You're no longer trying to be infallible.
You're in the unknown.
—Paul Arden, from *It's Not How Good You Are,*
It's How Good You Want to Be

Art House

For 20 years at Life is Good, we have created almost every piece of art and editorial internally. Not long ago, we decided we should be less restrictive. We decided to swing the doors open and collaborate with artists from all walks of life. We're excited about this. We call it our Art House Strategy. This new way forward embraces art in all its forms, including visual art, music, film, animation, poetry, theater, and more. It's the best way we know to bring people together to share new ideas, beauty, and inspiration. It's the best way we know to build a community of people who believe life is good.

Your own creativity, regardless of your age or passions or profession, can benefit immensely from the simple act of sharing your ideas openly and welcoming collaborative opportunities with a wide variety of creative people and groups. You'll find that 1 + 1 can

Fest friends team up to help kids: (from top)
The Avett Brothers, Sara Bareilles, Dave Matthews,
and Jack Johnson.

indeed equal 3, and a PB and J sandwich is much greater than the sum of its parts. Connect, collaborate, and create. It works inside the art world, and far beyond.

All Together Now

Creativity is a tool used by everyone from waitresses to engineers to customer service reps. It's not just an artist's tool; it's an everyday superpower. In most fields of work, at any level, there is room for approaching tasks with an eye toward creative improvements (in efficiency, product design, environmental sustainability, and more).

Our Life is Good operations team in New Hampshire is constantly finding creative ways to serve the business and move us forward. A classic example was their unorthodox answer to an urgent puzzle a few years back. As our LIG Festival was fast approaching, we found ourselves dangerously shorthanded for volunteers. For a fest weekend itself, we've always had a strong surplus of willing volunteers, but not so much for the pre-fest prep weeks of taxing, weekday setup labor. Our leaders reached out to a local program that paired prison inmates with volunteer opportunities. The following week we had a workforce of eager inmates assisting with the heavy lifting that got our farm site ready for an event that raised over a million dollars for kids in need. The inmates themselves, openly drawn to the purpose of the event, brought a focused dedication to their work. Our ops team (which creates and delivers answers every day) had once again used creativity to find a solution that benefited all.

Art for All Mural: Festival attendees paint freely on individual tiles that will magically become one unified piece of art.

FUEL:
CREATIVITY

IN-Q is a National Poetry Slam Champion. He writes to inspire and challenge his audiences to look deeper into the human experience and ask questions about themselves, their environment, and the world at large.

Superpowers by IN-Q

When I think of superheroes
I think of superhuman
I think of Superman
Wolverine and Wonder Woman
Usually they have a cape
Or a mask to hide their face
Just in case
They have X-ray vision and superhuman strength
Some can even breathe in outer space
They fly around a while but always come back to keep our
cities safe
They're here to save humanity from itself
It's a metaphor for how we look outside ourselves for help

And while the fantasies are fun
I choose to look to me and you
We don't need superheroes
We have superpowers too

It starts with being OPEN to the moment
If we do than we can own it

Besides it will be gone before we know it so don't blow it
We owe it to this second of eternity to show up
Embrace the possibilities and slow up
Take a breath and look around
See the sights and hear the sounds
Feel the ground
Notice there's a reason that you're in the now
You could be anywhere and yet you're here
When you accept it as your own you begin to overcome
your fears

And real COURAGE is looking in the mirror
It's deciding what you want to do
Then making it appear
Innovating out of thin air
You must be doing something right if you are scared
Otherwise you wouldn't care
It's a process to get from here to there
You're on the journey and you're learning
But building muscle means your gonna feel the burning

So SIMPLIFY it
Don't deny it
Try it
See if it can work for you
Change perspective to get a different view
And don't forget you gotta laugh at the truth

Cause sometimes a sense of HUMOR is the only thing
That pulls you through
It's medicine when you can let it in
An attitude of GRATITUDE is rising up from within
So even if the storm clouds block the blue from your sky
You'll remember that the sun is waiting for you on the
other side

And having FUN is something you must decide
From the lows to the highs
It's all a part of the ride
I can throw my hands up or hold on for dear life
But I'd rather live once then make the same mistake twice

COMPASSION is my passion
Empathy is my gift
But my growth is incremental as my consciousness shifts
So I CREATE from the abyss
Turning pain into gold
I'm an alchemist
An OPTIMIST and an AUTHENTIC soul

I believe that Life is Good
Even when it hurts to see
I believe in superpowers
And I believe in you and me
I believe in superheroes but I don't look for them flying
above
Cause they exist inside of us all and WE save the day
with LOVE.

Life
is Good®

THREE WAYS TO TAP YOUR CREATIVITY

1. **MIND YOUR SPACE.** Home, office, home office, studio, open-floor environment, or tight quarters: Wherever you do your thing, that physical space is also your mind space. Your mind feeds off of the look, sound, smell, and feel of it. Take a few fresh chances in your home or work space with colors that lift your mood and inventiveness. The common, "safe" fallbacks tend to be neutrals, but beige surroundings can foster beige feelings and ideas. Who wouldn't cancel a full day with beige to go to a meeting with green, or a party with yellow? Think through all the choices for your other senses too, and "feed your creativity."

2. **EXPLOREATE.** No, it's not a word, but it should be—because creativity is an exploration. Physically explore your world to ignite the creative spark. For The Beatles, that meant exploring planet Earth. If you have that luxury, go for it. But if not, exploring your hometown can do the trick just fine. Kids need unstructured time to develop their imaginations and their own ideas, and so do adults. If we pack our calendars from wake to crash, our creativity becomes mush, crushed beneath the weight of checklists.

   Choose a subject you love: dogs, sports, cooking, dance, the ocean, history. Whatever it is, get out and read about it, listen, watch, touch, and above all, *do*. There's nothing wrong with exploring a bit online, but we're talking about getting hands-on in the real world here. Hit the bookstores, back roads, mom-and-pop restaurants, lectures, and acoustic cafés. There is inspiration all around you, especially when you dial your mind in on a subject you love. "Not all who wander are lost" applies to your mind as much as your body.

You can't use up creativity.

Life is good

3. **TEAM UP.** Creativity is not something to keep to yourself. In fact, the more you use it and share it, the more you have. Make the time to dig into your garden or toolbox, or reconnect with the crafting or guitar strumming that makes you happy. And let it double as a social bonder by inviting others to join you. Not only does creative collaboration elevate your output, it builds quality bonds and trust. Connect, collaborate, and create.

TICITY

BE THE PERSON
YOUR DOG
THINKS
YOU ARE

You Had Me at Woof

Dog lovers share a special connection with Life is Good—they always have. They're some of our most loyal supporters. We created Rocket (the Life is Good dog and Jake's trusty pal) in 1999, and as he's grown and evolved through the years, so has our strong bond with a wide and passionate community of people with canine companions. They send us photos and write to us about their four legged friends as daily reminders that life is good. Letters are sometimes signed by "Lucky," "Zeus," or "Oreo," with very few spelling errors. There must be some natural connection between optimism and dog owners. Employee dogs of all sizes roam free in our offices.

> Who feels it knows it.
> —Bob Marley

Dogs teach us so much if we're willing to heed their wordless wisdom. Surely the greatest teacher in the "school of authenticity" is a slobbering ball chaser with a perpetually wagging tail. Always watchful, never judgmental, dogs love without reservation. And they're just as comfortable with who they are, too. Wide-eyed wonder comes easy when your tastes are simple and your mind is open to the joy of the moment. Dogs don't worry about the past or the future. Their focus is fixed on the present, and faults are forgiven faster than the flick of a Frisbee. They're always game to connect. Dogs not only accept what is, but they celebrate it whole-heartedly. They're never too proud to ask for what they need, and they're always at the ready when we need them.

Watching a dog run is a lesson in losing yourself in the moment. And in so much more, as Jonelle Rabeler describes in this moving letter:

FUEL:
AUTHENTICITY

Dear Life is Good,

Dagger, my beautiful golden retriever, is the epitome of your message and product, and he reminds me now how to live every day of my life. He was laid to rest yesterday under a beautiful maple tree near the woods at our house at six years old, after being diagnosed with cancer two weeks ago. He was not only my best friend; he was the best friend of everyone he came into contact with, because he saw the potential in everyone as his new buddy.

This morning, when it was so hard to get out of bed for the first time without his head on my side of the bed nudging me, saying "Come on! It's time to get up and see what adventures are in store for us today!" I looked at his picture and collar on my nightstand and knew that he would want me to remember that life IS good, and that he would want me to greet each day as he did.

When I'd take his Life is Good leash off the hook (no matter how quietly I'd do it, he always came running!), he could barely contain his excitement at taking the same walk we took every day. A hike, off-roading, or snowshoeing in the woods on a trail were his favorite activities, and he would run ahead (never too far) and then run back wondering what was taking us so long. With his beautiful smile he seemed to be saying "There are so many exciting things to be explored up ahead!"

Dagger was always in the moment: the wind blowing on his face in the backseat of the car, camping, rolling around in the snow, lying in that one spot where the sun happens to be shining at that moment. But really, as long as he was with his family, he was happiest no matter what we were doing. He possessed the best qualities that every human should aspire to: unconditional love, gentleness, loyalty, friendship, and enthusiasm for the simple things in life.

Cancer took my best friend too soon, and life may not always be fair. But it cannot take away that life is good. While Dagger won't be there to greet me at the door anymore with his enthusiastic smile and his wagging tail, I know that he is running carefree on a beautiful, tree-lined trail somewhere, full of excitement, turning to run back once in a while, waiting happily for me to catch up and explore the wonderful things ahead.

Jonelle

Grow Your Own Way

We all aspire to greet each day like Dagger. To run like a dog. To live genuinely, authentically. We want to stay true to ourselves, feel comfortable in our skin, and express ourselves naturally. We also want to live consistently in sync with our strongest values. "This above all: to thine own self be true," said the quotable Willy Shakespeare. But it can be a real challenge when external influences pressure us to be someone we're not.

Be yourself.
Everyone else
is taken.
—Oscar Wilde

It happens to all of us. As our business began to pick up steam in the late 1990s, we found ourselves getting more advice from experts about what was right for us. They told us, for example, that word of mouth was great for our start-up phase, but we had reached a point where more traditional advertising was necessary if we wanted to elevate our little brand. Who were we to know? So we started getting ready to do a series of radio ads.

One night in the spring of 1999, we found ourselves prepping for our first ad by reading aloud the script prepared by an agency. In addition to product hype, the proposed ad included terms like "made in the shade" and "party" as a verb. It described summer as "the season for the good life," and implied that our own lives were now good because business was growing. Then we got to the final line: "If you're looking for the good life, you *can have it all*, at lifeisgood.com." We almost yacked on the spot. We passed on the advertising, and we're thankful we did. It just wasn't us.

That decision helped open up our minds—and our funds—to pursue new ideas for connecting with people (like pumpkin festivals) that felt a little absurd but a lot more authentic.

Know Who You Are and Act Like It

From our earliest days, we dreamed of building a lasting company that people could trust and believe in. We've never been big on trendy marketing terms, so we made up our own simple definition of branding many years ago: *Know who you are and act like it.*

Many customers have skin in the game when it comes to helping LIG spread the power of optimism.

It works for us. If you're real, people can trust and believe in you. Simple and true. Authenticity is a superpower.

After 20 years in business—a period that coincides with the rise and explosion of the Internet—we've come to understand something else about brands. In today's world, businesses don't build brands. Consumers do. Consumers are in charge like never before. They have access to the information and they're savvier than ever.

Stay True

They can tell who's real and who's not. Consumers are connected and they talk—online and off. If people view your business as fake, they will tear you down. If they view you as authentic, they will build you up. Life is Good has never been the fastest, the strongest, or the smartest, but our customers have built our business with us because they know we're real.

A Community of Optimists

When we started, we got our feedback directly from customers on the street. Later, and still today, we listen closely to our retail partners. We're also a part of a rich, ongoing conversation through social media, where a growing community of optimists connect through Facebook, Twitter, Instagram, Pinterest, and more. We launched our Facebook presence late, but discovered very quickly that our expanding tribe was eager to engage. Our Facebook family is now 2.5 million strong. For two guys whose favorite app remains chicken wings, that's a pretty big number, and it's growing every day.

Those Facebook likes are more than fist bumps for the quotes we post or the products we feature. Our digital community lets us know what they like or don't like about what we're up to, often serving up helpful suggestions as well. They're part of the journey. They're co-creating the brand. They've grown to trust us, letting us into their lives, and they're happy to help us spread the power of optimism. They face adversity themselves, and they value reminders of what's right with the world. They share their own personal stories as well as the things that make life good for them. And they let us know that our social mission matters to them, too. Many dig into our website to learn what Playmakers does with the 10 percent of profits we donate. Others are happy with the simplicity of knowing that when you do business with Life is Good, you help kids in need.

We all appreciate authenticity, in people as well as organizations. We're drawn to the real deal, folks who actually walk the talk and are comfortable in their own skin. So how can each of us stay grounded in our core beliefs, even as we grow and evolve? How do you "know who you are and act like it"? A few possible answers lie ahead.

TEN SOLID SONGS OF AUTHENTICITY

- "The Story" Brandi Carlile
- "Little Room" The White Stripes
- "Born This Way" Lady Gaga
- "Rusty Old American Dream" David Wilcox
- "I Am Not My Hair" India.Arie
- "Like a Rolling Stone" Bob Dylan
- "Unwritten" Natasha Bedingfield
- "75 and Sunny" Ryan Montbleau
- "Respect" Aretha Franklin
- "The Once and Future Carpenter" The Avett Brothers

Connection Found

Personal stories are powerful. We learn a lot from them, and others do too. The Moth is a nonprofit group that organizes storytelling events all across the United States. One storyteller at a time stands on stage with nothing but a microphone and shares a personal story. Think about entertainment today. Stunning visual effects are created through a host of multimedia tools. Yet every week, around the country, the crowds flock to live storytelling venues, and millions more listen to the popular national broadcast of *The Moth Radio Hour* to hear a lone human being telling a story.

LIKERS GONNA LIKE

Humans have been doing this forever, haven't we? In caves, huddled around campfires, at the dinner table, or in the wee hours of the after-party, when the stories get especially colorful. Telling each other our tales. Making sense of ourselves.

We listen for many reasons. People's lives fascinate us, and we relate to them. We want to know what makes them tick. The stories reveal their character; their struggles, mistakes, choices, and consequences all serve to show us who they are.

When Life is Good reached its tenth birthday, we thought it made sense to celebrate the milestone. For the first time, we wrote a three-line version of our early years (or "heritage story") and included it on the hang tags attached to every piece of clothing we sold. It was a one-year plan. We questioned putting our history on the tags, because many businesses have a humble start, and we didn't think ours was so

special. But then our retailers and customers told us what it meant to them. How they connected to the story of two regular guys stumbling their way along and forming a company based on their beliefs. They liked the fact that we're still running the company too. The story is important to people because it's authentic, they told us. Keep sharing it. So we do. It's not rocket science. We listen, and try to deliver what people want.

You have a "heritage story" too. Each of us has a unique journey marked by experiences that shaped who we are. Reflecting on those formative stories occasionally can sharpen our understanding of where we came from, where we struggled and fell down, what we learned, and what we have come to value most. And when you share your story openly with others, they get to know who you actually are. These shared, authentic stories help us all build trusting relationships.

Reality Show

"Even your best friends won't tell you, but your mother will . . . You STINK!"

Sound like a friendly dose of optimism from our amazing mom? It was actually a standard callout to Joan's four sons when we each hit puberty and the need to employ deodorant became abundantly apparent. She laughed, she sang, she lifted our spirits daily—but like all good parents, she could also clock us right between the eyes with the truth.

We all have blind spots. To deepen self-knowledge and stay true to yourself, it's invaluable to have people close by who know you well enough to tell you the truth. As brothers, we've grown up and worked together for a long time. We have no problem calling each other out and keeping each other honest. Familiarity and trust make directness—straight talk—a bit easier to give and take.

That's the way it is with the Life is Good online community. You see our flaws, our missteps, and you let us know. We heard you loud and clear on issues with too many "generous" cuts on our shirt styles, and it led us to design a broader variety, including many fitted options. The company is imperfect and always will be. Its founders are even more flawed. When driving, John has been known to miss (not one, but up to) three exits while his mind wanders, and car speed varies wildly. Bert continues to type with a single finger—not classic hunt-and-peck style with a single finger on each hand, but literally with one finger. We're both technically inept. The list goes on. But our values, like our wardrobes, haven't changed since high school. People tend to be forgiving when they know you're listening, you're trying, and your aim is true.

As hard as it is to hear sometimes, straight talk from the people closest to us is a gift we can't find elsewhere. It's free of sugarcoating, and it helps us keep growing while staying true to ourselves. If you're fortunate to have some close, tell-it-like-it-is people in your life, welcome their constructive criticism as well as their praise— because that combo (versus pure hugs and high fives alone) makes you stronger.

Early Admission

My mistake. My bad. My fault. Strong words that cut the tension when things go wrong, and help us all move forward. Authentic people work to understand their own weaknesses. That's not always easy, but let's face it: No one is perfect (except for Morgan Freeman as Red in *The Shawshank Redemption*). In fact, true authenticity that creates deep trust includes exposing vulnerability, acting with humility, and admitting when we drop the ball.

One big mistake we made nearly sunk our young company back in 1999. We fell in love with a shirt sample from a local supplier who had a relationship with a factory in Pakistan. Back then, annual sales were about two million bucks. We ordered a shipment of 20,000 shirts. Their delivery was supposed to kick off our year in January, and we took an exciting number of orders with our key accounts. But the shirts never showed up. The delays and shipment promises from the factory went on for four months. The problem was we didn't know the people who owned this factory. We didn't even know the supplier very well. We just loved the quality of the shirt, so we thought we'd take a shortcut.

Finally, we had to call our accounts to apologize. We kept it short and sweet. No, call it short and bitter. We personally called every customer and told each of them that we screwed up. They could easily have said to us "You're telling us you can't give us T-shirts for *months?*

Run like a dog.

YOU'RE A T-SHIRT COMPANY!" And then they could have walked away. We could hardly blame them. Instead, they told us they appreciated our honesty. They knew who we were, and they trusted us to get things right in the future. We had screwed up pretty badly, but we fessed up. We lived to ship another day because authenticity (inside and outside business) goes a long way. And since that day, we always take the time to build relationships with the people who make our products.

Stay True

We can take a lot of genuine inspiration from our favorite pets. Some days we may even envy our dog, cat, or horse because they're rolling on pure instinct, enjoying the simple things, and living in the moment. Their treats might

FIVE LESSONS IN AUTHENTICITY WE CAN ALL LEARN FROM DOGS

- If you want something, ask.
- Don't judge. Just love.
- If it looks fun, go for it.
- Squirrels are fast.
- Wag and the world wags with you.

even taste better than ours, for all we know. They definitely have some inside jokes on us. You can see it in their eyes.

For humans, staying in the moment and honoring our deepest values is a daily challenge and a lifelong quest. Perfection is not achievable on this quest, but improvement always is.

Staying true to ourselves requires a curious mix of self-awareness and self-abandonment. On the one hand, it takes dogged determination to openly acknowledge our flaws and keep striving to improve. On the other hand, trusting your instincts, tabling introspection, and hitting the trail at full stride like Dagger can feel like the ultimate expression of our best self.

THREE WAYS TO KEEP IT REAL

1. **TAKE A STAND.** Expressing yourself takes courage. Especially when you're the odd vote, the oddball, or the odd bird. It can also be liberating to fly free of consensus, especially when you speak positively. "Irony is the easy way out," says musician Jack White. "It's an anti-opinion, an opinion without taking any chances." It's too easy for people to deride, or declare only what they're against. What are you FOR? Take a stand. When you do, you invite others into real conversations—and that's where authentic relationships are born.

2. **GET LOST, GET FOUND.** Lose yourself in the flow of your favorite activity—be it basketball, yoga, gardening, or trail walks with a friend. It's one of the best ways to refresh and reconnect with the real you.

3. **TUNE IN.** Ask three people closest to you to share with you two things that they hope will never change about you and one thing they believe could use a change. Doing so will help you discover your genuine strengths as well as focus on a key area where—could it be?—you have opportunities to grow stronger.

be
you
tiful

Nothing Is Stronger

Sometimes people think Life is Good is just about hanging out at the beach on perfect, sunny days. But optimism is actually most valuable—and most powerful—on darker days.

New England is steeped in rich traditions, and one of our favorites since childhood is the Boston Marathon. The race always takes place on the third Monday of April, and it is the oldest annual marathon in the world—118 years and counting. Screaming fans who've been cooped up all winter line the 26-mile course from Hopkinton, Massachusetts, to Boston's historic Back Bay neighborhood. The sprawling scene is always ultrafestive. Parties on front lawns and rooftops, BBQs on stoops, music in the air, and wall-to-wall people spilling into the streets to sing and dance and cheer on the runners. It's a special day to be in the city. Perhaps the pièce de résistance is the homemade motivational signage: "Wicked Hahd but you gaht this, Mah!" or "Cold one waitin' for ya, Uncle Billy!"

From 2004 through 2014, our headquarters were right in Boston's Back Bay, only a couple of blocks from the finish line. So our employees could walk right out the door to cheer on friends in the race. Later in the afternoon, we'd all meet up on our roof deck on Newbury Street for a cookout. We're pretty simple people, so looking around at the smiles on the faces of lifelong friends and co-workers on Marathon Monday was always a nice slice of the American dream for us.

On April 15, 2013, however, that dream became a nightmare. The Boston Marathon bombings and subsequent related shootings killed four innocent people and badly injured more than 200. The Back Bay streets became a sea of panic and chaos. The bomb detonations resounded loudly through our office, drawing our team to the fifth-floor windows above the street in time to see people running and cops descending on the scene. We got on our cell phones and gathered all of our crew back at the Life is Good offices so we could make a count. When the dust settled, we were missing one.

Our good friend and colleague John Banse had been standing near the second of the two bombs, and he was hit. We went straight over to Mass General Hospital, where they were operating on him, but were unable to get any information about his condition because we are not immediate family. Understandably, the hospital was crawling with heavily armed military forces, which was actually comforting to see at the time. (People often complain about the military and the police until we need them.) In the wee hours of the next morning, we were asked to leave the hospital. We left not knowing whether our friend was going to live or die. "We expect he'll live," was the exact quote from a surgeon. Not particularly comforting.

Once the sun was up, we went back to the hospital and they let us in to see our friend. He didn't look pretty, but he was alive and talking to us. It's hard to express the relief we felt at that moment. The bombs used in this hideous act of terror were pressure cookers packed with nails and ball bearings. The doctors had spent the night removing as much of the homemade shrapnel as they could, literally from John's head to his toes. His body was covered with wounds, he had third-degree burns, his left Achilles tendon was half-severed, and both eardrums were ruptured. Yet all things considered, he was one of the fortunate ones, and he knew it. In a true show of his character, minutes after we entered his hospital room, he said, "I'm grateful." Those seemed like odd words coming from an innocent victim of a violent crime. He later explained that he had seen some of the other victims, so he was glad to still have his life and all his limbs.

we

not
me

While the police spent the rest of the week successfully hunting down the bombers, we needed to focus on the rest our team's health at Life is Good. Many of our employees were shaken up by what they had seen and heard, and by the fact that one of our own teammates was suffering. Over the next few days, we made sure trauma counselors were available to everyone, and we tried to spend lots of hours together as a group. Meanwhile, "Boston Strong" became the popular slogan in the streets. It was a powerful message of unity and resilience. People took pride in the idea that the terrorists had messed with the wrong city. Many other clothing and sports companies began producing "Boston Strong" T-shirts, so our customers and staff naturally began asking if we would produce them as well.

It was very tempting to do just that, but then we felt there might be an opportunity to make a different kind of statement. We met with some of our team to discuss what a brand called Life is Good should say in such a moment. It wasn't an easy conversation. No matter how we sliced it, two young men had chosen to commit a horrific crime whose aim was death and destruction. All major media outlets were making sure we saw those bombs exploding over and over and over again. The hate story was being told everywhere we looked. But there was another story unfolding too—a more powerful one.

Seconds after the bombs exploded, people were performing acts of love. The EMTs and other first responders to the scene, the people who lent their phones or welcomed strangers into their homes, the runners who pushed themselves beyond marathon distance and ran to nearby hospitals to give blood, the medical staff that worked 40- or 50-hour shifts. And what happened after the first few days passed? The love only grew. People donated services to expedite creation and delivery of custom prosthetics; musicians donated their time and talents to raise spirits and money. People from around the globe sent caring letters and prayers, opening their hearts and their wallets to help. It was an outpouring of love.

Yes, two young, very confused men committed horrible acts of hate, and we can't reverse that. But following those acts, and as a direct reaction to those acts, millions of people performed acts of love. The Boston Marathon bombings showed two human beings at their worst and millions of human beings at their best. We talked about all of this as it was happening. And we realized that love was the real story.

> People can you feel it? Love is everywhere.
> —*The Allman Brothers Band*

So we created a T-shirt that said "BOSTON" on the front with a small heart in the center of one of the O's, and the words "Nothing is stronger than LOVE" on the back. We weren't sure what the reaction would be. We weren't even sure if most people would understand it. But our team really got behind it. They jumped into action, and 30 hours after conception the shirt was for sale in stores and on our website. And people did understand it. Much to our amazement, BOSTON LOVE became the best-selling T-shirt we've ever made. In less than 60 days, that one T-shirt generated over half a million dollars in profit. And we donated every penny to The One Fund, established to help the victims and their families.

In response to the 2013 Boston Marathon bombings, Life is Good put the focus on Love to help heal survivors.

We're proud of our friend John Banse for turning to the super-powers courage and gratitude when he needed them most. (We love you, buddy!) We're proud of all of our retail partners who stepped up to sell the shirts, and of our team at LIG for working so hard to produce and deliver the goods. Nothing can ever heal you completely from a day like that. But working together to help the victims and their families helped us move forward. We're proud of the resilience of our tough little city, too. Boston banded together at a very difficult time. But most importantly, we're proud of humanity for choosing love over hate.

Love is a superpower.

> Action is
> eloquence.
> —William
> Shakespeare

Love Is Action

We can express our love authentically in words—from a sincere "How are you?" or "How can I help?" all the way to "What the hell are you thinking?" (tough love). But sometimes love needs no words. The aftermath of the 2013 Boston Marathon made this so clear. Love is action. Deeds. Selfless acts. Follow-through. It's being there not just when you're asked, but also when you're not asked.

We have a friend who was shoveling snow off a neighbor's rooftop. He accidentally fell through a skylight, smashing both his forearms in an attempt to brace his fall into the high ceiling kitchen. Both arms were in casts for several months. Among many physical challenges, one was standard cleanup duties after using the bathroom. His girlfriend at the time never hesitated to perform the honors when her man was on the bowl. "That's love," they both told us with a smile. They've now been happily married for many years—and it's clear that either of them would always step up (or down) to do anything for the other.

After all these years and a million efforts, poets and songwriters are still finding ways to express love in new ways. Thankfully, that will continue. In our daily lives, we sometimes need reminders of the power of love—a word we can never say, hear, sing and spread enough. We're also wise to remember that our actions—and often, our mere presence—can speak even louder.

In the digital age, "Be here now" is a tall order, making its fulfillment all the more meaningful to our relationships. It can be for a kid's practice, a relative's birthday, or a random Tuesday night when a friend just needs some face time.

Human beings are social creatures. We need love to reinforce our deep connection to each other. When we receive a good hug, a warm smile, even a heartfelt high five or fist bump from someone we love, the positive result bolts right past our brains and goes straight to the heart. We feel one with the larger tribe of humanity. When you can provide that emotional charge for others, it can be even more rewarding.

TEN POWERFUL SONGS OF LOVE

- "Blue Sky" The Allman Brothers Band
- "Ho Hey" The Lumineers
- "Make You Feel My Love" Adele (Bob Dylan cover)
- "Same Love" Macklemore & Ryan Lewis
- "Anna Begins" Counting Crows
- "I Wish" Stevie Wonder
- "Love You Madly" Cake
- "Better Together" Jack Johnson
- "Good to See You" Neil Young
- "Hey Jude" The Beatles

FUEL:
LOVE

Dear Life is Good,

This is a story of love, hope, and acceptance.

In April of 2010, my mom decided that holding and loving babies was her calling. She became a foster parent in order to give respite to babies who have been taken from their parents with the hopes of reunification or adoptive placement. My husband and I are really happy she did, because shortly thereafter, we met the most amazing person who has changed our lives forever: our son Eamon. His home with us was his fifth home in his nine short months on this planet.

Having met later in life, my husband and I had given up hope of having a family when this beautiful little soul entered our lives. We became certified and worked at transitioning him into our home. He was very shy and delayed in many areas. But through the gifts of love and patience, Eamon has grown into a confident and happy little boy.

Almost 18 months from the day we met Eamon, this past Tuesday, we finalized our adoption and our forever family was created. Life is Good is part of our forever family too.

Warm regards,
Tanya, Brad,
and Eamon

Do What You Love Love What You Do

Words to Live By

Our tagline to the left is a good one, don't you think? It's simple, fun, phonetically playful, and memorable. But it's far more than just a tagline. It's a way of life. And it's our single most important piece of advice to share with the world.

Life is Good has always been less about us, and more about the receivers of the message. As a result, the feedback we have received from our customers has always paved the way. Our customers have co-authored the story of Life is Good. We don't dictate the exact meaning of our messages. Instead, our messages are always open to interpretation. We just throw ideas out there to get the conversations started, and then we listen and watch to see where folks take it. The best insights become part of our brand. That's why we never feel like we're selling something. We always feel that the LIG community owns this movement with us. From optimists who have inspired us through the years, here are a few things we've learned about "Do What You Love. Love What You Do."

Dear Bert and John,

Do What You Love. Love What You Do. I noticed that both of these two short sentences use the exact same four words, but since the order of the words in each sentence is different, the meaning of the sentences becomes very different to me. Does that make sense?

"Do What You Love" reminds me to sing. I'm not a good singer, but I love to sing anyway. There is nothing in this world that makes me happier than singing. I have a Life is Good towel in my bathroom with the words "Do What You

Love. Love What You Do" on it, and it gets me singing in the morning. Singing puts a bounce in my step on my way out the door.

The "Love What You Do" part is just as important to me. It reminds me not to be so hard on myself. Life is not easy for me. I have had real challenges in my life. But I'm trying. I still make mistakes, but I don't dwell on them the way I used to. Instead, I focus on my progress, and that calms me down. I'm not perfect by any stretch, believe me. But I'm a better person than I used to be. And I'm proud of who I am today. I honestly couldn't say that in years past. My friends today are my friends for life, and my students count on me to be there for them.

So for me it all boils down to this: I know I have my best days when I let myself sing a little, and I know I improve the most when I allow myself to be my own biggest fan. I know these things, no question about it, but I sure do appreciate the reminder on my orange towel.

Sincerely,

Tiara

Schoolteacher, Chicago

Most people we hear from perceive "Do What You Love" to be about action. It says "Do," not "Say," so that makes sense. It seems to tell people not to think so much all the time. To relax the mind and do what feels good. Your body is wise. Listen to your body. If your body wants to run, run!

"Do What You Love" tells some people to go mountain biking or fishing, do yoga, take a nice walk in the woods with their dog, play football, or go for a refreshing dip in the ocean. We are physical creatures and we sometimes forget that in the digital age. Our bodies were made to move.

"Do What You Love" tells other people to read a great book, create a delicious meal, get your hands dirty with some gardening, or play guitar. These may seem like little things, and they are at the time we are doing them. But for more than 20 years now, we've heard folks from all walks of life tell us over and over that regularly doing what they love has an enormous impact on their energy, their self-image, their performance at work, their coping skills, the health of their relationships, and their overall happiness.

Many tell us that "Love What You Do" is about pride in one's actions—in other words, living in such a way that when you look back on your actions, you feel satisfaction. That view requires a wide-angle lens. It's about living a fulfilling life, a life with purpose.

FIVE FILMS DISGUISED AS CHICK FLICKS RECOMMENDED BY TWO DUDES FOR ALL DUDES

- *Love Actually*
- *Amelie*
- *(500) Days of Summer*
- *The Five-Year Engagement*
- *About Time*

In recent years, we have been inspired by Generation Y, "the Millennials." Never before had we interviewed people for positions at Life is Good who ask more questions about our nonprofit work than they do about our for-profit work. They want real purpose in their lives, and they're not shy about it. They ask about our vision for making the world a better place before they even ask how much the job pays. They want to make a difference. Millennials are our kind of people. They seem determined to Love What They Do. We're fired up about the quality of people coming our way.

Some people see the words as advice about career paths, like Ted, a recent college graduate who interned with us a few years ago.

Hey LIG!

It's me Ted! How's everybody doin'? Do you miss me? I can't believe you're able to stay in business without me. JK.

I also can't believe it's taken me this long to write you about the idea that has changed my life. I had worn LIG T-shirts since I was a kid, and I must have read the words "Do What You Love. Love What You Do" a thousand times, but the real meaning went right over my head. I only associated it with simple pleasures, like having a cookout or going to the beach.

I was a business major in college, but I struggled in courses like Stats and Finance. I was never very good at math. Accounting was the worst for me. In between my junior and senior years, I looked into switching out of the business school altogether, because I just didn't know if I was cut out for it. It was too late to switch majors though, and that's when I took the internship with you guys. Thank God for that because it made me realize there is a great place for me in business. I may not be a numbers person, but I am a people person.

I absolutely loved working in the Human Resources department at Life is Good. Human Resources is all about helping people, and that's what I'm all about. I had never really looked forward to working before. I don't know if most people do. But it surprised me when I was in Boston that I really looked forward to working every day. What a great feeling. While I was up there, a friend asked me how I liked what I was doing and the words just popped out of my mouth, "I love what I do." "That's so cool," my friend said. "Having a job where you love what you do and you actually get paid to do it would be the ultimate. That's what I want." For me, that's now the real meaning of Do What You Love. Love What You Do. I can't believe I never realized that. Am I stupid? Don't answer that. I'm on a roll.

I am now working in recruiting at a great tech company down in Raleigh, North Carolina, and every day I am helping other people to Do What They Love and Love What They Do. Yeehaaaaa!

Ted
Former LIG Intern

Hello Life is Good,

I'm writing you today because I've had an epiphany in my life, and it relates to your slogan, Do What You Love. Love What You Do.

For years, I would try to stay motivated by saying these words to myself, "Be the best husband you can be. Be the best dad you can be. And wherever you work, be an irreplaceable asset to the company."

They were noble thoughts, but it really wasn't working. I wasn't a bad husband or dad or leader at the office, but I was frustrated because I knew I could do better. I was *trying like mad, but I was just not myself. I was uninspired, and at times it was obvious. I was even embarrassed by it. I was always happy and inspired as a single guy. I love my wife and kids—I never had second guesses about that. But I just wasn't happy a lot of the time and I couldn't fig- ure it out. My company is awesome too, and there are huge opportunities for me to grow here. But I wasn't happy at work either.*

You're going to think I'm crazy when I tell you this, but I figured it out, and here's what I say to myself now: "Be selfish." That's right! Be selfish. Why? Because giving myself completely to my family and my work wasn't work- ing for me. My quantity of giving was high but my qual- ity of giving was low. I didn't have joy and enthusiasm myself. I didn't love myself. So how could I give love and joy and enthusiasm to my family and to my work if I didn't have those things myself? The answer is I couldn't. This was like the sky opening up for me.

So I sat down and thought about the things I used to love to do that I gave up in pursuit of being a great dad and husband and employee. They were all things I just didn't think I had the time to do anymore, and things I thought I could easily do without. On the top of my list was playing soccer. I had played soccer com- petitively since I was nine years old. Soccer is part of who I am. I love the game, and I gave it up cold turkey at 27. I am also a movie nut. I love comedies and science fiction and I love to go to the theater, but I hadn't been to a movie since I got married. What was I thinking? And finally, but most importantly, I lost all contact with a few close buds from college who actually don't live far from us at all. That wasn't a conscious decision, but I also wasn't consciously trying to do the things I love, like hanging out with them, so I just let it slip.

Anyway, I talked with my wife about all this, and she is just plain smart. She knew I was barking up the right tree. She knew this was going to be good for all of us, so she smiled at me and said, "Go for it." I joined a local men's soccer league last fall and I'm going to play on another team in the spring. I'm not in the best shape, and my skills have waned a bit. But running on that field and having teammates is incredible. I can hardly express what playing again has done for me. Just putting on a uniform is magic. When I come home from playing, I am super dad! And every other Wednesday I go to the movies, sometimes with my wife, and sometimes with one of the guys I lost touch with. The stress goes away and I let the movie take me to some place cool. I love my movie night. I feel like I'm born again because I'm doing the things I love.

Never change that slogan for your company. Do What You Love and Love What You Do. I live by those words. My goals were to be a great father and husband and employee. Life is never perfect, but today I can honestly say I'm getting it all done. Who would have thought the best way for me to accomplish my goals was by chasing a ball around a field and watching movies?

Thanks for the wake-up call,
Ben

Spread It Like Peanut Butter

We will never forget the outpouring of love our city received in the aftermath of the Boston Marathon bombings. Love is there for us when we need it most.

But love can be light, too, and it's available to us every day. There are entire shows, blogs, books, and campaigns devoted to what infuriates people, what they hate. (We believe in free speech, but how many venting outlets do we really need?) On the other hand, how refreshing is it when somebody speaks from the heart about something they love? Bluegrass, blue fishing, or blueberry pie: The subject matters far less than the personal passion. The world needs more love, and when you share what you love, it brings people together.

Our friend Packy loves grilled cheese sandwiches. Our dad loves mountains. Our sister Eileen loves deep ocean dives, and Berta loves to paint. Our brother Ed loves space exploration (sometimes in mid-conversation). And Allan? He loves to laugh with everybody—especially his wife and four daughters. Everybody loves, but not everybody shares what they love enough. What do you love? Seriously, who and what do you love?

The more you share your love, the more you connect with the people you love—and the more you connect with the people you love, the richer your life is. The recipe is time tested, and it will never change. So go ahead, spread it. Love is a superpower. Don't keep it in a jar. Spread it all around like peanut butter, because life is good.

THREE WAYS TO SPREAD THE LOVE

1. DO WHAT YOU LOVE. LOVE WHAT YOU DO. Allow yourself to step back and take a broad view of your life. Write down the things you love to do most. Then ask yourself, are you doing what you love? Are you loving what you do? If you're like most people, the answer is, "sometimes." And that's not bad. Next, guess what percentage of the time you are doing what you love. Same for loving what you do (however you choose to interpret that). Over the next 30 days, try to move the needle by 10 percent. Just by monitoring your actions, you will make positive strides. Write down what changed and how you feel, then continue to use these simple words as a guide to make big or small adjustments in your life.

2. TAKE YOUR LOVE EVERYWHERE YOU GO. Choose someone you love very much, and honor that person by bringing him or her with you everywhere. Many people put pictures of a loved one in their wallet or on their phone display or screensaver at work. Keeping them in your heart and front of mind helps frame your experiences from a foundation of love. Let's say you choose to bring your daughter with you. You'll be surprised how she might change your mood on a long commute, or in a meeting that's dragging on. Carrying the people you love with you at all times can help carry you through even your hardest days.

3. EXPRESS YOURSELF, TODAY. Love is not a power to reserve for our greatest emotional peaks and valleys. Unique occasions like weddings, birthdays, as well as funerals, tend to naturally crystalize love—but it's too powerful to hold back from our daily interactions. Express it today through your words AND your actions—because even among superpowers, nothing is stronger.

Take your love
everywhere you go

After

JOAN'S GOODBYE

Joan's Goodbye

In 2006, we realized that the old home at Sunnyside Road, where our parents still lived, was truly dilapidated. It was also far too tiny to entertain all the new munchkins coming along in the next generation. Free of us freeloaders for well over a decade now, it was an empty nest, but it was far from empty. Our dad, a lifelong collector of books, had filled every conceivable nook with deep archives on mountaineering, architecture, Churchill, FDR, chess, oceanography, bridges, trains, radio telescopes, and a thousand other favorite topics. The house appeared to be buckling under the weight of all its paper tenants. We finalized plans with the family to build our folks a spacious, new home on the same lot. But first we had to raze the house where we were raised.

Our versatile brother Ed stepped into the role of demolition and architectural strategist, as well as general contractor. When the day arrived to actually knock down the old homestead, we assumed it would be an emotional moment for our mom. After all, she had raised her entire family and lived most of her life under that roof. But you never really know what to expect with Joan, and on this day she surprised us.

In their high school years, our older brothers Ed and Allan had been notorious for sleeping in and skipping morning classes. In their defense, they were both working long hours by night to assist with family bills. Their old bedroom dormer was on the left, jutting out from the roof on the second floor. When the demolition foreman offered Joan the chance to take the first swing with the excavator bucket, she stepped into the cab like an old pro. After some basic lessons on the controls, and with the bucket already poised at dormer height, Joan tilted back with a smile and shouted, "Time to wake up, boys!" followed by a swift, crushing blow to the dormer.

Joan gets fired up for demolition in Needham, Massachusetts, 2006.

We all howled as she stepped down from the digger, fist waving high in triumphant pumps.

She put the old behind her and embraced the new. It was classic Joan. She faced change in a healthy, courageous way, with open arms, a big smile, and a pretty good punch line to boot.

The new, roomier home built on the site of the old house was completed in 2008. It seemed to breathe new life into our dad and prompted far more gatherings as well. Al had mellowed through the years, and his relationship with all of us was stronger than ever. We were in a good place. Even the label "The Bear," which was only whispered in the old days, was now an affectionate nickname we openly shared with him. He had transformed from grizzly to teddy bear.

In the new house, Dad became a lot more sociable, and Mom had some space to paint and play with her grandkids. "I never knew your dad was so funny," friends said. "What's gotten into him?" During a conversation late one evening, The Bear told Ed that he felt as though he missed 25 years of his life. "It's strange," he said, "I just don't remember those years very well." Still, he was now more relaxed and happier than we had ever seen him, and that's what was important to us.

Sunday pancake breakfasts at Sunnyside became a favorite new tradition for all of us. It really took us back to see Joan crawling around the floor like a wild lion as she acted out the characters from whatever book she was reading aloud to her grandkids. These years

would truly prove to be among the best for Joan and Al, filled with lots of quality family time among the three generations.

By 2013, Joan was still flying around the house playing Quidditch with the grandkids and loving her exercise classes at the senior center twice a week. She was 86 now, but she was no old woman. Her mother had lived to be 102, and all signs looked like she was on the same program.

It came as a shock to all of us in November of that year to learn that Joan had stage four lung cancer. She had never smoked a cigarette in her life. In family huddles, we explored various treatment

Friends and family surround Joan and The Bear at the new house on Sunnyside Road in 2010.

options, but the cancer was moving quickly throughout her body.

She tried a few rounds of radiation. As she was leaving for her treatments, she'd give us a big smile and say, "They're doing their best to remove the termites. Wish me luck!"

Ultimately, she chose to prioritize the quality over the quantity of time she had left with us. When word spread that she was on her way out, we heard lots of great things about our mom from people who knew her well. A woman named Brenda Sweeney told us something we'll hold dear forever: "I grew up with your mother in Jamaica Plain [an old neighborhood of Boston]," she said.

"I've known her since the third grade, and she's the only person I've ever met who's never said a bad word about anybody."

Joan never wasted time denigrating others or wishing for things she didn't have. Even as the cancer spread through her lungs, and

Joan and The Bear enjoy a good laugh with one of their grandkids.

into her spine and brain, there was grace, and her ever consistent savoring of the little moments that made her life so rich.

As her condition worsened in the weeks that followed, we took the time to sit with her and ask if there was anything she had always wanted to do but never got the chance to experience. Someone she always wanted to meet, someone she needed to talk to, or some special place she always wanted to go?

She thought for a little while, but then answered with great certainty. "I am scared about the cancer," she admitted, "but aside from that, I've never been happier in my life. I've got everything I need right here. I just want to be surrounded by you kids and the little ones too."

We were a bit frustrated by her answer. We wanted to be her heroes. Maybe fly her over the Grand Canyon or get her a front row seat at a Broadway show. How about a trip to Paris? We wanted to proudly grant Mom her final wish. But how could we do this if she wouldn't ask for anything?

After discussing it a few times, we realized why she didn't need to scramble or make amends. She didn't have anything she needed to make up for, because she had lived her life just the way she wanted to. Joan had loved with all her heart, every day of her life.

The next day we drove to Sunnyside, and instead of asking her what she wanted again, we told her we understood, and we explained our theory. "That's fine," she said, in a matter-of-fact tone, "but I did think of something." Haaaaah! Of course she did, right? "Not while I'm alive," she continued, "but after I go, and after the funeral, I want you to throw me a good party." Joan loved parties.

One of Mom's favorite memories of her youth, often retold with a beaming glow, was seeing big band icon Glenn Miller's orchestra play in the 1940s at a classic old ballroom called the Totem Pole. In January 2014, our brother Ed learned that a top-notch, full-scale Glenn Miller cover band was playing locally.

We made plans to take her in a small bus packed with loved ones, including her two sisters, both in their 80s as well. The day before the dance date, Joan became extremely disoriented and unable to walk. She was rushed to the hospital, experiencing nausea and hallucinations. We pulled the outstanding Dr. Friedman aside that afternoon, and asked him if a bus trip and dance hall date the following night made any realistic sense to him. "Quality of life," he replied. "It's beyond worth it to try. If your mother is coherent and still game tomorrow, I say you give it a go."

TEN SONGS OF OPTIMISM

- "What Light" Wilco
- "Wavin' Flag" K'NAAN
- "Hold On" Alabama Shakes
- "Here Comes the Sun" The Beatles
- "Honor and Harmony" G. Love & Special Sauce
- "Bleeding Out" The Lone Bellow
- "A Change Is Gonna Come" Sam Cooke
- "My Silver Lining" First Aid Kit
- "Three Little Birds" Bob Marley
- "Soulshine" Warren Haynes

We boarded the bus the next night and cranked up the big band tunes all the way. When we arrived at the old school dance hall, it was clear the time machine had dropped us off in the right era. A polished 18-piece orchestra was up front with horns wailing. Joan, as fate would have it, was remarkably lucid, laughing, singing, and dancing to her old favorites. She danced with her sisters, kids, friends, strangers, and herself at times. She was fully immersed in the moment, soaking in the familiar sounds and all the love that surrounded her.

When our brother Allan told us Joan's sister Sheila had "hit the wall" around 10:30, we acknowledged it might be time to get the octogenarian trio to their beds. Then Allan clarified: Sheila had literally rocked back on her chair laughing and hit the wall—*with her head*—while watching the dance scene. Fortunately, we looked back to find Sheila already recovering with a floppy ice pack on head, swaying to the beat and now flanked by her two giggling sisters.

One morning a few weeks later, the whole family got an urgent message to get to our parents' house immediately. Joan's health had taken a sharp downward turn. The Bear, 92 at this point, was sharper than ever—but it's not often that he puts a freshly ironed shirt on. When we got to the house, the way he had shaved and dressed up was a small symbol of his love for Joan. He knew this was it.

All of us circled around the bed that day to say goodbye to our mom. She was the best mother any person could ever want. It was a special gift that she didn't suffer long, and that we had that precious opportunity together to be with her in her final hours. We did our best to tell her what she meant to us, impossible as that was to describe in words. The grandkids told her they loved her too, and asked her not to leave. We sang—poorly as ever, but from the heart—every song we could think of that she might enjoy: "What a Wonderful World," "Chattanooga Choo Choo," "Lean on Me," "Stand by Me," "Let It Be." It morphed at times into a roast of wandering parody songs, the silliness bubbling up to try to ease the collective pain and sorrow. We had no idea if she could hear us or not, but they say you should keep trying, because you never know.

It occurred to us that The Bear and Joan should have some private time, so we cleared out the room. They had been married for 57 years, and they had been through a lot together.

We checked in on them once or twice, and he was talking with her. It's a beautiful memory we have of him, holding her hand as she passed from this world.

Joan was the powerful optimist right to the end. In her final four months, after her initial diagnosis, she had shown us once again how to handle adversity. She channeled courage and gratitude to remain focused on the good, to celebrate and enjoy what she still had (which in her view was everything). She illustrated that a life lived authentically can end with grace and peace. And what can we say about love? Joan bathed in it and kept spreading it right to the very end. Joan *was* love.

Joan's wake and funeral were followed immediately by a moving and decidedly festive celebration that, we can only hope, fulfilled her one simple request. We could hear her wild laughter echoing that night—and thankfully, those who knew her always will.

The time to say goodbye to this world will come for all of us. When it does, will we need to run around to make up for love we didn't give? Or will we sit back and smile like our mom did, and say, "Throw me a good party"?

The Time of Your Life

When we are younger, everyone tells us we need more of everything. More education, more clothes, more money, more stuff. But as we get older, we all come to realize that the only thing we need more of is time. Time to do the things we love, and time to be with the people we love.

Choose what you do with your time very carefully, and protect that time with your life, because it *is* your life.

Rallying Cry

We often joke with each other that we only have one skill in this world: We're good at making friends. It's not really a joke, though. Without that one skill, we'd probably still be sleeping in our van.

The mission of Life is Good is to spread the power of optimism. That's our story, and we're stickin' to it. And that story has only just begun. We get to keep sharing this adventure with you. There are a lot of wild and unpredictable chapters yet to be written together. Our story is your story, and vice versa.

So bring it on! As a community of optimists with superpowers, we are capable of anything—and we want to see and hear anything you have to show and tell. We want to learn from your best days and your worst days. How do you, and the people you know and love, kick your superpowers into action?

We want to hear from all the friends we've met along the way. And as our good friend Ryan Montbleau sings:

Most of all, this one goes out to the ones we've yet to meet.

We hope you've enjoyed this book, and we hope it has shown you how optimism can bring more joy and meaning to your life. Joan and Al Jacobs taught their kids to say please and thank you . . . so please, be good to each other, and thank you for spreading good vibes.

Acknowledgments

Thank you to our publisher National Geographic for convincing us that if we included lots of cool artwork, we could write a book.

Thank you to our stellar editor, Hilary Black, and our good friend and writing coach, Jim Laughlin, for showing us how to actually write a book, and to the talented design, editorial, and production team at National Geographic: Jonathan Halling, Melissa Farris, and Anne Smyth.

Thank you to each one of our talented and dedicated co-workers at Life is Good for spreading good vibes every day.

Thank you to each of our old friends who sold T-shirts with us in the streets.

Thank you from John: To my bride Jess and our three little monkeys, for your superpowerful love.

Thank you to The Bear, Eileen, Berta, Ed, and Allan for allowing us to expose all the shocking Jacobs family secrets.

And finally, thank you to every person who has ever written us a letter or an email, sent us a photograph, drawing, poem, or a song, bought a Life is Good product, given a Life is Good gift, or suggested an idea or a change to us. You inspire us. You are Life is Good.

Your friends,
Bert & John Jacobs

Notes

Introduction

11 **strong link between optimism and increased mental and physical health . . . higher overall quality of life** Emily Esfahani Smith. "The Benefits of Optimism Are Real." *The Atlantic*, 2013. Accessed April 23, 2015. Available online at http://www.theatlantic.com/health/archive/2013/03/the-benefits-of-optimism-are-real/273306/.

Simplicity

88 **Digital screens, including smartphones, make falling asleep harder and lead to less restful slumber** Stephanie Sutherland. "Bright Screens Could Delay Bedtime." *Scientific American*, 2012. Accessed April 23, 2015. Available online at http://www.scientificamerican.com/article/bright-screens-could-delay-bedtime/.

Humor

94 **Laughter has therapeutic value and promotes overall health and wellness . . . strengthens our immune system** "This Emotional Life: Benefits of Humor." PBS.org. Accessed April 23, 2015. Available online at http://www.pbs.org/thisemotionallife/topic/humor/benefits-humor.

Gratitude

126 **strong links between gratitude, mental health, and well-being** Amy Morin. "7 Scientifically Proven Benefits of Gratitude." PsychologyToday .com. Available online at https://www.psychologytoday.com/blog/what-mentally -strong-people-dont-do/201504/7-scientifically-proven-benefits-gratitude. *Further Reading:* Amy Morin. *13 Things Mentally Strong People Don't Do: Take Back Your Power, Embrace Change, Face Your Fears, and Train Your Brain for Happiness and Success.* New York: William Morrow, 2014.

126 **reported that grateful people are happier . . . and they have stronger coping skills for the challenges and setbacks they experience** Michael G. Adler and N. S. Fagley. "Appreciation: Individual Differences in

Finding Value and Meaning as a Unique Predictor of Subjective Well-being."
Journal of Personality, vol. 73: 1 (2005), pp. 79–114. Accessed March 27, 2015.
Available at DOI: 10.1111/j.1467-6494.2004.00305.x. Alex M. Wood, Stephen
Joseph, and John Maltby. "Gratitude uniquely predicts satisfaction with life:
Incremental validity above the domains and facets of the five factor model."
Personality and Individual Differences, vol. 45: 1 (2008), pp. 49–54. Accessed
March 27, 2015. Available online at http://www.sciencedirect.com/science/
article/pii/S0191886908000767. Alex M. Wood, Stephen Joseph, and Alex P.
Linley. "Coping Style as Psychological Resource of Grateful People." *Journal of Social and Clinical Psychology*, vol. 26: 9 (2007) pp. 1076–1093.

Compassion

167 **neuroscientists have confirmed that our brain exhibits a similar pain response to another's suffering as it does to our own** Emile
Bruneau, Nicholas Dufour, and Rebecca Saxe. "How We Know It Hurts:
Item Analysis of Written Narratives Reveals Distinct Neural Responses to
Others' Physical Pain and Emotional Suffering." *PLoS ONE*, vol. 8: 4 (2013).
Accessed April 24, 2015. Available at DOI: 10.1371/journal.pone.0063085.

167 **when we give to or help others, a circuit in the brain is activated and
makes us feel good . . .** L. B. Aknin, E. W., Dunn, G. M. Sandstrom, and M. I.
Norton. "Does social connection turn good deeds into good feelings? On
the value of putting the 'social' in prosocial spending." *International Journal of Happiness and Development*, vol. 1: 2 (2013), pp. 155–171. Accessed
April 24, 2015. Available at DOI: 10.1504/IJHD.2013.055643. Jordan
Michael Smith. "Want to Be Happy? Stop Being So Cheap!" NewRepublic
.com. Accessed April 23, 2015. Available online at http://www.newrepublic
.com/article/119477/science-generosity-why-giving-makes-you-happy.
Further Reading: Christian Smith and Hilary Davidson. *The Paradox of
Generosity*. New York: Oxford University Press, 2014.

167 **In the 1950s, the skeletal remains** "What does it mean to be human?" Smithsonian National Museum of Natural History. Accessed April 23, 2015. Available
online at http://humanorigins.si.edu/evidence/human-fossils/fossils/shanidar-1.

Photo Credits

All images courtesy Life is Good unless otherwise noted:

105, Doug Smathers; 111, Mark W. Mercer; 120, Tim Gray; 122-3, Ryan Mastro; 138-9, Rich Gastwirt; 141, William James Warren/Science Faction/Corbis; 150, John L. Davenport; 152-3, Mark W. Mercer; 154-5 (UP), Straub Collaborative; 154-5 (LO), Aimee Corrigan; 155, Michael D. Spencer 2011; 156, Straub Collaborative; 157 (LO), Straub Collaborative; 158, Will Wohler; 163, Allison Shirreffs; 172, J. R. Thomason, Association for Play Therapy Annual Conference, 2012; 196 (UP), Aimee Corrigan; 196 (CT LE), Rich Gastwirt; 196 (CT RT), Straub Collaborative; 196 (LO), Aimee Corrigan; 199 (UP), Michael D. Spencer 2011; 199 (LO) Mark W. Mercer; 235, Joe Burke; 255, Andy Jagolinzer.